Democracy, Inequality and Economic Development

Democracy, Inequality and Economic Development

Edited by

C. Vinodan

Co-ordinator, Rajiv Gandhi Chair for Public Policy Studies
and
Honorary Director, Institute for Contemporary Chinese Studies (ICCS), School of International Relations and Politics, Mahatma Gandhi University, Kottayam, Kerala

New Century Publications
New Delhi, India

NEW CENTURY PUBLICATIONS
4800 / 24, Bharat Ram Road,
Ansari Road, Daryaganj,
New Delhi - 110 002 (India)

Tel.: 011-2324 7798, 4358 7398, 4101 7798
E-mail: indiatax@vsnl.com • info@newcenturypublications.com
www.newcenturypublications.com

Editorial office:
LG – 7, Aakarshan Bhawan,
4754-57/23, Ansari Road, Daryaganj,
New Delhi – 110 002

Tel.: 011-4356 0919

First Published: **2018**

ISBN: **978-81-7708-445-0**

Published by New Century Publications and printed at Milan Enterprises, New Delhi.

Designs: Patch Creative Unit, New Delhi.

PRINTED IN INDIA

About the Book

India is a federal parliamentary democratic republic. The Constitution defines the organization, powers and limitations of the Central and State Governments.

India has a multi-party system, consisting of various types of national as well as regional political parties. Political parties represent different sections and regions and play a major role in the politics of India. Through the electoral process, the people of India choose their representatives to run the government.

There is a widespread perception in the country that disparities amongst states, and regions within states, between urban and rural areas, and between various sections of the community, have been steadily increasing in the past few years. The gains of rapid growth witnessed in recent past have not reached all parts of the country and all sections of the people in an equitable manner. That this perception is well-founded is borne by available statistics on a number of indicators. Widening income differentials between more developed and relatively poorer states is a matter of serious concern.

Livelihood options in rural areas are also limited as agriculture does not provide adequate returns and industry is virtually absent leading to limited trade and services. People seeking employment in low skill and hence low paying jobs is a common manifestation of these constraints in many rural areas.

In short, the pattern of economic development over the years has left in its trail a variety of inequalities which have caused socio-politico tensions.

The present volume contains 11 papers—authored by scholars in the field—which provide an in-depth analysis of various issues confronting the Indian economy, and how they are to be resolved within the democratic framework of the country.

About the Editor

Dr. C. Vinodan is currently Co-ordinator, Rajiv Gandhi Chair for Public Policy Studies and Honorary Director, Institute for Contemporary Chinese Studies (ICCS), School of International Relations and Politics, Mahatma Gandhi University, Kottayam, Kerala. He has worked previously at the Post-graduate and Research Department of Political Science, Sree Narayana College, Kollam and Department of Political Science, University of Kerala.

He obtained his M.A. (II Rank), M.Phil. and Ph.D. degrees in Political Science from the University of Kerala. He was awarded the Visiting Scholar Fellowship (2003) by the Claremont Graduate University, California, USA. He has attended numerous courses in international relations in India and abroad. These include the 2016 Sino-Indian Cross-Cultural Dialogues held by the Institute of Advanced International Studies, Sun Yat-sen University, Guangzhou, China; and the US Department of States Fulbright American Studies Institute (FASI) course on foreign policy at the University of Delaware, Philadelphia in 2000.

Dr. Vinodan has also attended and presented papers at various national and international conferences/seminars. He is also the recipient of a number of awards including Kerala University Post-Doctoral Award (2003-2005). He is also a member of the editorial board of the *Journal of Human Security*, *Indian Journal of Politics and International Relations* and *South Asian Journal of Diplomacy*. He has published 40 research papers and 4 books.

His areas of teaching and research activities include international relations, security studies, Chinese studies, South Asian studies, energy, environment and human security.

Contents

Contributors

G. Palanithurai	Professor, Department of Political Science and Development Administration, The Gandhigram Rural Institute, Dindigul.
Mirza Asmer Beg	Professor, Department of Political Science, Aligarh Muslim University (AMU), Aligarh.
J. Prabhash	Professor and Head, Department of Political Science, University of Kerala, Thiruvanathapuram.
A. Mohanakumar	Associate Professor, Department of Political Science, Devaswam Board College, Sastamcotta, Kerala.
Shaijumon C.S.	Assistant Professor, Department of Humanities, Indian Institute of Space Science and Technology, Thiruvananthapuram.
Divya Balan	Guest Lecturer, Department of International Relations and Politics, Central University of Kerala, Kasaragod.
Rishika Chauhan	Ph.D. Candidate, School of International Studies, Jawaharlal Nehru University (JNU), New Delhi.
John S. Moolakkattu	Professor, School of Gandhian Thought and Development Studies, Mahatma Gandhi University, Kottayam.
Nisha V. Nair	Dr. S. Radhakrishnan Post-doctoral Fellow in Economics, School of Gandhian Thought and Development Studies, Mahatma Gandhi University, Kottayam.

C. Beena University Librarian (i/c), Cochin University of Science and Technology, Kochi.

Sajimon Abraham Faculty, School of Management and Business Studies and Honorary Director, University Centre for International Co-operation (UCIC), Mahatma Gandhi University, Kottayam.

C. Vinodan Co-ordinator, Rajiv Gandhi Chair for Public Policy Studies, School of International Relations and Politics, Mahatma Gandhi University, Kottyam.

Rajeev M.M. Assistant Professor, Department of Social Work, School of Social Sciences, Central University of Rajasthan, Ajmer, Rajasthan.

Praveen Kumar Associate Professor, Centre for Political Studies, Central University of South Bihar, Gaya, Bihar.

Preface

India is a constitutional republic governed under the world's longest written constitution, federally consisting of 29 states and 7 Centrally-administered Union Territories (UTs).

Democratic Set Up

Politics in India takes place within the framework of its Constitution, as India is a federal parliamentary democratic republic, in which the President of India is the head of the country and the Prime Minister of India is the head of the government. India follows the dual polity system, i.e. a double government which consists of the central authority at the centre and states at the periphery. The Constitution defines the organization, powers and limitations of both the Central and State Governments, and it is well-recognised, rigid and considered supreme, i.e. laws of the nation must conform to it.

There is a provision for a bicameral Union legislature consisting of an Upper House (called the Rajya Sabha), which represents the States of the Indian federation and a Lower House (called the Lok Sabha) which represents the people of India as a whole. The Indian Constitution provides for an independent judiciary which is headed by the Supreme Court. The court's mandate is to protect the Constitution, to settle disputes between the Central Government and the States, inter-state disputes, to nullify any central or state laws that go against the Constitution and protect fundamental rights of citizens, issuing writs or their enforcement, in case of violation.

The governments, Union or State, are formed through elections held every five years (unless otherwise specified), by parties that claim a majority of members in their respective lower houses (Lok Sabha in Centre and Vidhan Sabha in States). India had its first general election in 1951, which was won by the Indian National Congress, a political party that went on to dominate the successive elections up until 1977, when the first non-Congress government was formed for the first time in independent India. The 1990s saw the end of a single party domination and rise of coalition governments. The elections for the 17th Lok Sabha, held from April 2014 to May 2014, once again brought back single party rule in the country, with the Bharatiya Janata Party (BJP) being able to claim a majority in the Lok Sabha.

Role and Types of Political Parties

Compared to other democratic countries, India has a large number of political parties. There are many types of political parties in India: national and regional. Every political party must bear a symbol and must be registered with the Election Commission of India. Symbols are used in Indian political system as an identity of political parties so that illiterate people can also vote by recognizing symbols of the party.

India has a multi-party system, where there are numerous national as well as regional parties. A regional party may gain a majority and rule a particular state. If a party is represented in more than 4 states, it would be labelled as a national party.

As with any other democracy, political parties represent different sections among the Indian society and regions, and their core values play a major role in the politics of India. Both the executive branch and the legislative branch of the government are run by the representatives of the political parties who have been elected through the elections. Through the electoral process, the people of India choose which representative and which political party should run the government. Through the elections, any party may gain simple majority in the lower house. Coalitions are formed by the political parties in case no single party gains a simple majority in the Lower House. Unless a party or a coalition has a majority in the Lower House, a government cannot be formed by that party or the coalition.

Problem of Inequalities

There is a widespread perception in the country that disparities amongst states, and regions within states, between urban and rural areas, and between various sections of the society, have been steadily increasing in the past few years and that the gains of the rapid growth witnessed in the recent past have not reached all parts of the country and all sections of the people in an equitable manner. That this perception is well-founded is borne by available statistics on a number of indicators. Widening income differentials between more developed and relatively poorer states is a matter of serious concern.

While differences in per capita income are summary economic indicators of disparities, there are wide variations among the states even on other parameters like health, education and infrastructure. In the current scenario, where high growth rates have led to a spiral of commercial and service sector activities in the already developed regions, the backward areas continue to lack even basic amenities such as education, health, housing, rural roads, drinking water and electricity. Livelihood options are also limited as agriculture does not give adequate returns and industry is virtually absent leading to limited trade and services. People seeking employment in low skill and low paying jobs is a common manifestation of these constraints in many rural areas. Compounding these problems is the lack of manpower to man essential services such as educational institutions and health centres. A large part of the disparities is probably due to historical reasons, differences in initial conditions and natural resource endowments.

While the above is the situation as between states, very much the same picture is seen as amongst the different districts and regions within the states. Even in highly developed states, there are regions and districts whose indicators are comparable to those of the poorest districts in the most backward states. While some level of intra-state and inter-state disparity is bound to exist even in the best possible situation, the effort of the policymakers must be to enable backward regions to substantially overcome the disadvantages they suffer from and provide at least a certain minimum standard of services for their inhabitants.

In short, the pattern of economic development over the years has left in its trail a variety of inequalities which have caused socio-politico tensions.

I take this opportunity to place on record my deep sense of gratitude to all the contributors to this volume. Their scholarly contributions provide an in-depth analysis of various issues confronting the Indian economy, and how they are to be dealt with within the democratic framework of the country.

C. Vinodan

1

Democracy and Decentralization of Power in India

G. Palanithurai

This work is based on author's experience of working with communities and institutions with the aim of promoting equality and dignity for the poor and marginalised through the process of democratization and decentralization. It is realized that wherever the poor and the marginalised are facilitated by either civil society organizations or academic institutions, transformations are visible. Equality and dignity have been achieved. But these achievements are through a process of prolonged struggle. It has been demonstrated that there is no short cut and it is only through a process of struggle and for which democracy facilitates.

The whole transformative process of the communities and groups has been captured in this article. While capturing the real life stories, focus will be given as to what extent academics can play an effective role in democracy promotion activities. This is captured with a view to demonstrate that the higher learning institutions can perform the third dimension of the academic activity namely outreach or extension which is missing in Indian higher learning institutions. If higher learning institutions are involved in outreach activities, communities around the institutions could be transformed easily.

Introduction

Indian democracy is being viewed with much appreciation by the scholars in the West who specialize in democracy promotion because of the struggle it undergoes for sustaining the minimum values of democracy through the electoral process. This appreciation is not because of the quality of democracy that India maintains. It is because India maintains a minimal form of representative democracy continuously with a break of two years despite the play of an array of negative socio-political forces and practices against democracy. [1] Maintaining a minimum set of democratic values in India is not a simple task as India has more anti-democratic social practices which are vibrant and active in all spheres and activities of the communities in India. [2] It is an irony that even in political parties one could not see healthy democratic practices despite the stipulation imposed by the Election Commission of India.

Only a few political parties are practicing democratic values in their functioning. Many in fact wanted to evade from these practices. Even after sixty seven years of democratic practice, we are in minimal democracy [3] as per the standardized classification done by the scholars and also in institutional democracy.

Democracy is always in dynamic form and it evolves in different patterns in the world. [4] Tokenism and symbols are visible. In India, the struggle is to transform the institutional democracy into a behavioural democracy by changing the attitude, belief, and behavioural traits of the people towards the values, and norms of democracy. The core values, namely equality, liberty, freedom, justice, fairness, equity, respecting the dissent voice are not in social and political practices. [5]

Having understood the nature and structure of Indian society, M.K. Gandhi rejected the adoption of Western model of representative democracy for governing the Indian society. He anticipated that this institution will be used to exploit the people by a few who are able to sneak into the governing system. [6] Hence, he outright rejected the Western model despite the whole-hearted support extended to this model by a dominant segment in the intellectual group among the founding fathers of modern India. Yet, it has been adopted as creating a centralized nation-state; the option of many of the liberated societies from the colonial yoke after the Second World War.

When the whole world was moving towards centralized state system, M.K. Gandhi advocated a decentralised governing system with the active participation of the people. It is also an irony that the intellectuals of the world took nearly forty years to realize the potentials of decentralization. Only after four decades of experience in democratic governance, many of the governments felt that the big government approach has not delivered the public goods effectively and the world has to move towards an alternative governance system to meet the unmet demands of the people. [7] In that context, 'decentralization' was considered as the best option to manage the resentment of the people over the poor performance of the state. [8] India is one among sixty countries which has entered into a big pang approach. India opted the path of constitutionalising the process of decentralization to move on a different path of democratization. [9]

The Context

First time in Indian democratic governance history, a vibrant participatory local governance mechanism has been created through an amendment to the Constitution of India. It is historic and path-breaking in terms of its potentials to bring revolutionary changes in the socio-political and economic life of the poor and the marginalised provided the potentials are being understood by the stakeholders who are going to get benefits out it. The whole process of transformation would take place only through a democratic process. The decentralization process and democratization process are complementary to each other. [10] The two processes require enormous input from various segments of the society to produce the intended results. Because what has not been achieved in the past through big government approach, has been fixed as the basic objectives of the new dispensation.

The 73rd Amendment to the Constitution of India has promised economic development and social justice to the poor and marginalised. It will be achieved through a participatory democratic process with the involvement of the stakeholders in the process of governance and development. The above objectives appear to be simple but to realize the same, a mass movement is necessary and unless otherwise a mass movement is in place it is only rhetoric and not a reality. Even after twenty years of practice of new local governance system in India, many are in search of reasons for the slowdown of interest in decentralization at present.

But Jayaprakash Narayan made a path-breaking analysis in his address at the Annual Conference of All India Panchayat Parishad conference in Bangalore after the demise of Nehru on the obstacles for decentralization of powers. [11] In this article, what I intend to do is to investigate as to what extent the decentralization process has been achieved through a democratic process by leaving out the analysis of the impact of decentralization in the communities at the grassroots. While doing so, I will highlight what a higher learning institution can do for democracy promotion and deepening activities through the experience of a Department in a small university.

The Challenges

Decentralization and democratization in a society which is diverse in character and known for its inequality and inequity have to face challenges and stiff resistance. Both provide opportunities to the hitherto marginalised and excluded communities and groups to participate in the process of governance and development. If both are understood broadly and perspectively, one will find the potentials to bring fundamental changes at the community level. It requires a thorough preparation and massive mobilization of the poor and marginalised to make use of the new opportunities. This process is not free from obstacles and barriers. [12] This is so because the new dispensation works for transfer of power from the dominant to the marginalised, men to women and from bureaucracy to the elected representatives. People who are at the helm of affairs know that this Constitutional amendment will not allow those who enjoyed power so far to be in power forever. They know the full implications of the power transfer and as a result those who have been in power so far evolve new designs to keep power with them. 'Elite capture' has come in decentralization discourse because of this syndrome. Groups which are going to get advantage out of it have to make themselves aware of the new possibilities and opportunities that come through this new dispensation and organise themselves to take on the new opportunities.

However, the above task is through a process of struggle. The struggle is also a long drawn struggle and for which poor have to be prepared and facilitated. Who will facilitate the poor and who will be part of the struggle of the marginalised groups to make use of this opportunity is the question. In this regard, academics have to play a crucial role from awareness creation and conscientisation to extending handhold support to the poor women, and other marginalised groups elected to the local governments. Theoretically speaking, middle class has a role in the transformative process of the society. Amending the constitution is only a necessary condition for the establishment of a permanent local governance institutional arrangement at the grassroots. [13] But it is not a sufficient condition. Sufficient conditions are many.

First, a confirmative legislation has to be passed in the provincial legislature by confirming the spirit of the 73rd Amendment to the Constitution of India. The state government's Panchayat Act will reflect the will of the state government in devolving powers to local bodies and in responding faith in peoples' will and capacity. To operationalise the Act effectively, the state governments have to remove or amend the state acts which are having the provisions against the spirit of the 73rd Amendment and conformity legislation. Proper rules and by-laws have to be created and they are to be in place and are to be simplified. They should be in the form of a manual—an administrative manual.

Simultaneously, awareness has to be created among the stakeholders about the new opportunities. It is a kind of marketing of the products of a company. It should be done as a company does marketing of its product. It should be done in a mission mode by adopting a market approach. Media, judiciary, academia, civil society and opinion makers have to be conscientised and sensitized about the new dispensation and its implications. [14]

In one judgment, the Supreme Court of India equated the power of Gram Sabha with Lok Sabha. Research institutions have to oversee the proper creation of State Election Commissions and State Finance Commissions and their functions from the perspective of the spirit of the 73rd Amendment to the Constitution of India. The state government has to evolve a policy for capacity building and to create a new leadership school to transform the elected representatives into transformational leaders to bring transformation in the society. Because there is no training policy for training the elected representatives, the available training institutions barring a few are not in shape to train leaders. A support structure has to be created to extend handheld support to the local bodies to deliver services and discharge their responsibilities. The whole range of activities have to be done by various agencies and of them, state's role is pivotal.

By keeping the above matrix of operationalization of decentralization of powers, a state has been evaluated as to what extent steps had been taken to implement the 73rd Amendment to the Constitution of India. This evaluation requires not a mechanical process. It needs an organic intellectual analysis. It is not a verification process. It is an in-depth analysis. Scholarly exercise can alone bring the reality. Table 1.1 shows how a state has taken efforts to decentralize powers to grassroots institutions.

Table 1.1 Decentralization and Democratization in Tamil Nadu

S. No.	Item	State		
		Yes	No	Partially
1.	Conformity legislation	√		
2.	Amending contradictory State Acts		√	
3.	Rules for governance and administration			√
4.	Preparation of administrative manuals		√	
5.	Awareness about decentralization			√
6.	Creation of autonomous State Election Commission			√
7.	Conducting free and fair elections periodically			√
8.	Sensitizing media and making them aware of the importance of local governance			√
9.	Strengthening the capacity to do periodical research on local governance for creation of new knowledge on local governance			√
10.	Commissioning State Finance Commission periodically	√		
11.	Getting report from the State Finance Commission and acting on them			√
12.	Evolving capacity building policy		√	
13.	Conducting capacity building for elected representatives			√
14.	Capacity building for the officials			√
15.	Evolving micro plan for integrated development		√	
16.	Monitoring mechanism for smooth functioning of panchayats	√		
17.	Building support structure			√
18.	Building partnership		√	

contd...

19.	Implementing II ARC Report		√	
20.	Implementing Mani Shankar Aiyar Report			√
21.	Creating activity mapping		√	

Source: Computed from the works of the Rajiv Gandhi Chair for Panchayati Raj Studies, Gandhigram Rural Institute (Deemed University), Gandhigram.

Democratization

First time in Indian democracy, a constitutionally created democratic governance structure is in place at the community level through the 73rd Amendment to the Constitution of India. Till then, rural communities have been in the habit of following the community practices to regulate the affairs of the communities. One cannot expect that the whole community will change itself from following the archaic community practices to the provisions of the Constitution. It is an obvious fact that Indian society is feudal in character and following a hierarchical caste system with economic inequalities is ultimately reflected in the attitude and behaviour of the people. Against such socio-economic background, the new governance mechanism has to work at the grassroots.

There is yet another force—the bureaucracy—which all along has established its hegemony over the community down below the district level and now has now to work under the elected representatives. The bureaucracy is not free from the influence of the social system. Thus, an array of forces at the community level is working against the practices of democracy and in this context, the new governance mechanism has to deliberate and decide and allocate resources for the development activities. In rural areas, those who have been at the helm of affairs in the community system have to give space for the newly created constitutional bodies of governance. This process will face a lot of resistance, covertly and overtly.

Before coming to the main argument of implementing the new dispensation, it is an imperative to dispel the clouds surrounding the concept decentralization of powers. There are two kinds of operational definitions that have been given to the concept 'decentralization of powers'. One is broader and encompassing assigned and assumed roles and responsibilities by using the law of subsidiarity. The other is a narrower view of looking at decentralization of powers by treating the local bodies as institutions for implementing the schemes of the state and central governments. A narrower definition of decentralization of powers limits the potentials of the new local government. It has come for mere provisions of services alone. In reality, it has come for larger purposes. It has come for achieving economic development and social justice.

The above objectives have to be achieved through a new process. It is through a participatory process. In the participatory process, the affected, weak and the marginalised have to be involved as participants. To enable them to participate in the process of development, they have to be empowered. Arrays of steps have to be taken to prepare the poor, women and other marginalised groups to participate in the process of governance and development. Further, it has to be done with a perspective. The perspective is that the development of the marginalised is not based on charity but based on rights. Thus, rights perspective should be kept in the backdrop of the governance at the grassroots. Thus, broader conceptualization of decentralization is the need of the hour. It has to be given by the opinion makers and intellectuals who shape the public opinion. Otherwise, the bureaucracy will take the narrower and legal view of 'decentralization' which will not enable people to release the energy.

Power transfer will not happen without a struggle and it is a time consuming process. It requires not only the political support but also needs the broader support of the intellectuals, media and the masses. This struggle has to be waged through non-violent means as advocated by M.K. Gandhi for achieving *Swaraj*. In the process of power transfer, people who assume responsibility and leadership in the local bodies have to discharge functions not only the assigned ones but also the assumed ones. It requires a new kind of leadership. It should not be a conventional managerial leadership but it should be a transformational leadership. It should be a creative, vibrant, visionary and revolutionary leadership. Attitude, behaviour, and activities of the leadership should enable the people to repose faith and confidence in him or her.

Thus, this type of leadership has to be shaped. Electing a leader is in the hands of the people but shaping the leadership is in the hands of the leadership schools. Hence, transformational leadership training has to be organised to enhance the capacity of the elected representatives of the people. It cannot be performed by the conventional, state institute of rural development. It requires a new kind of institutions. It should be run not by the bureaucrats but it should be run by the intellectuals and visionary leaders. It requires training module, exemplary intellectuals and leaders as trainers and training ambience. It can be done only by the institutions of higher order with creative individuals.

A very important organ of democracy promotion is media. In the last five to six decades, media had been oriented to look at issues from the perspective of federal and regional governments and politics. But now the paradigm of governance and development has been changed from *top down* to *bottom up*. This new perspective needs understanding from media as they play a vital role in sharing and shaping opinion, perception and views of the public. Who will do this job is a major question. Media has to be sensitized and conscientised by the intellectuals of higher learning institutions. Enormous preparation is needed on the part of the academics and intellectuals in higher learning institutions.

A sound policy and programme of a government basically depends on sound knowledge base and sound knowledge base depends on a sound database. Unless we have sound knowledge base, we cannot expect a proper policy from the governments. Policy advocacy is being done at the federal government and regional governments level on several issues. In the same way, policy advocacy has to be done for grassroots governance also. Vastness of the country with regional variations requires state specific advocacies. To do the exercise from every state, a policy advocacy group is needed. Continuous research has to be carried out on all the issues and aspects of local governance and development. Very poor research output has been witnessed so far from the intellectuals of higher learning institutions and research institutions on local governance and local development issues. Still, 68 percent of the people live in rural areas. 58 percent of the people rely on agriculture for their livelihood. To look at the issues of the people in the rural areas from the perspective of local governance, we need more number of researchers from social science branch of higher learning institutions. Till today, we are not able to form collegiums of scholars to do research on the issues of rural local governance.

Micro level participatory planning is an integral part of the new paradigm of local governance. It is the missing aspect in local governance which is also a violation of a provision of the Constitution. Now it has been reinforced by the Fourteenth Finance Commission of India through its recommendations. Who will assist the panchayats to evolve a plan for development in the absence of a regular machinery of planning? It has to be done by the higher learning institutions. In India, database is weak and data collection process is not on a sound footing. Especially, data on poverty and households is utterly weak. But now, a new opportunity comes in the form of creating governance and administrative institutions on a permanent basis at every gram panchayat. By using this opportunity, a scientific database can be created at every administrative unit, especially on households. This could be done by the academic institutions.

To make rural local bodies more vibrant and efficient an array of steps are needed. For many of the activities, academic institutions especially higher learning institutions can play a proactive role.

Democracy Promotional Activities

From Gram Sabha to micro level participatory planning, all are mentioned only in the 73rd Amendment to the Constitution of India as concepts. They have to be operationalised in a broader context of decentralization and democratization. Creating mere democratic institutions will not bring a democratic culture in a society which has emerged in federal cultural moorings. Hence, all the institutions have to be enabled to transact their business through democratic processes and procedures. [15] In the rural local governance process, we have gram sabha, committees in village panchayats, village panchayat council, block panchayat council, committees in block panchayat, district ward council, district panchayat committees and district planning committees.

All these institutions have to take decisions, allocate resources, spend the amount, execute the decisions and evaluate their activities and its impacts. To perform all these activities, well laid procedures have to be evolved. These procedures have to reflect the core values of democracy. These procedures should reflect equality, respecting dissent voice, fairness and justice. From seating arrangement to allotting time to express their views in the meetings of all the institutions, procedures have to be evolved and they have to be followed not as a ritual but as letter and spirit. Of course, this process will bring disturbance in many of the rural areas. Ruling, dominance, suppression, oppression, obedience are the practices which are against equality.

Take the case of gram sabha. Gram sabha is the parliament of people at the grassroots. People should be oriented to participate in the Gram Sabha meeting. For enabling the people, certain basics have to be evolved. Gram sabha has certain mandatory functions and apart from the mandatory functions, it has to assume certain responsibilities to develop a culture of democracy. Gram sabha can be made as a discourse centre, a debating centre, a deliberation centre and a centre for dissemination of vital information on governance and development. Leading the members of gram sabha towards a discourse requires leadership. An effective, interesting and meaningful discourse in gram sabha depends on leadership. In such a way, the leadership has to be shaped. An informed and nurtured leader can alone lead a matured and informed debate in gram sabha.

In the Indian context, maintaining equality and dignity in the discourse of a forum is a difficult task. Like gram sabha, panchayat council meetings and panchayat committee meetings have to be conducted. In the Indian context, meetings have been made more of a ritual rather than for evolving a meaningful decision-making process after a thorough discourse and deliberation. This could be possible only by evolving a manual (guidebook) for the conduct of meetings prepared by intellectuals and others.

Select Observations of Gram Sabha Members

A Gram Sabha Member (Ms. Mariamma, 62 years old) in Karisalpatti gram panchayat in Dindigul District made the following observation: "Many of the government schemes are implemented by various departments and agencies in our village. Who in which office, implemented the schemes of the government, are not known to us. I have used gram sabha to track information. I got all the information only from the gram sabha. This is possible because of the observer coming from Government Departments to gram sabha and explaining to us. My close relatives have not received their old age pension for several months and she was not able to move out from her house.

When it was raised in the gram sabha, the gram panchayat president took responsibility to get details from the concerned office. Promptly, the president took steps to help the old women. As a result, she received her pension. I am a wage earner in MGNREGA, and I was not sure of getting wages on time. Hence, I raised this in the gram sabha meeting. I got the reply. I am an unskilled labourer working in a farm. Panchayat operates drinking water supply when I am in the farm. I raised it in the gram sabha. Since many of the women belonging to my shift raised the same timing of drinking water supply, it was changed to suit our requirements. To me it is a parliament. I got this information from our SHG meeting".

Mr. Muniasamy, a Gram Sabha member in Alamarathupatti Gram Panchayat in Dindigul District made the following observations: "Gram sabha is a best place to demonstrate equality in an unequal society. Caste hierarchy is a reality in the rural areas. Untouchability is yet another practice that operates in different forms in the villages. Gram sabha is an instrument to change the mindset of the people.

A dalit cannot sit along with the higher caste persons in any social functions in the village settings. But in gram sabha, I find that equality at least in sitting along with them. I regularly attend the gram sabha meetings only to enjoy that equality in the village by sitting with higher caste men and women. Everybody has to sit only on the floor.

Further, I can ask questions in the gram sabha. Questioning a higher caste person in a village in unacceptable. But in gram sabha being a president he or she has to respond to all the questions. I raise many questions and I get answers for my questions. I enjoy questioning. I enjoy sitting with a higher caste person. It gives joy and happiness. Being a dalit I can only realize the joy".

Here is a Model

Despite the promises of decentralization and performance of the rural local bodies in India, why political class and bureaucracy are not evincing interest in strengthening local bodies is a major question daunting in the minds of exponents of democracy and decentralization. There are many reasons and of them one is the failure of the middle class and intellectuals in performing their catalytic role.

In is context, I would like to dilate upon the activities of the Rajiv Gandhi Chair for Panchayati Raj Studies in strengthening panchayati raj in the last fifteen years. It is an account of voluntary activities evolved by a set of teachers in a small university by creating a chair in the Department. Rajiv Gandhi Chair for Panchayati Raj studies in the Department of Political Science and Development Administration, Gandhigram Rural Institute-Deemed University has been created only by the teachers in the Department. It was the first Rajiv Gandhi Chair in India. It was not given by the UGC. By seeing the voluntary works of the teachers many donor agencies have funded the activities of the chair. By seeing the activities of the chair, a few Members of Parliament have also contributed money to construct a building for the chair. In the whole of India, Rajiv Gandhi Chair of Gandhigram Rural Institute has got a separate building. It has carried out a wide range of activities to strengthen panchayati raj institutions in Tamil Nadu. An account of the activities in a nutshell are given in Table 1.2.

Table 1.2: Activities of the Rajiv Gandhi Chair for Panchayati Raj Studies

S.No.	Activities	Support	Coverage
1.	To create awareness among the people about new panchayati raj system.	Formed a network called Tamil Nadu Campaign for Panchayati Raj (TCPR)	The whole state. It conducted as an extensive work
2.	To exert pressure on the government to conduct the elections.	Submitted petitions to the Governor. Worked for inclusion of panchayat elections in the election manifesto of the DMK and TMC during 1996	
3.	To conduct voter awareness programme	With the support of PRIA and the Hunger Project, pre-election vote awareness programme was conducted by the chair with the support of a large number of civil society organisations	The whole state has been covered

contd...

4.	To conduct training programmes for elected representatives	Prepared training module with the support of CAPART and Rajiv Gandhi Foundation	For the whole state
5.	To conduct training programmes for elected women representatives	Prepared training module with the support of the Hunger Project	For Tamil Nadu elected women representatives
6.	To conduct training programmes for the dalit elected representatives	Prepared training module with the support of PRIA	For Tamil Nadu dalit leaders
7.	Leadership training	The chair conducted training programmes for 8,000 gram panchayat presidents. It was supported by CAPART, the Hunger Project and the Government of Tamil Nadu	For the entire state
8.	To assist the administration	Administrative manual has been prepared and published both in English and Tamil languages	For Tamil Nadu
9.	To sensitise and conscientise the media	Media workshops have been conducted with the support of the Hunger Project	Entire state
10.	Establish handhold support for women leaders	Elected women representatives' federation has been created and it was assisted by the chair	Entire state
11.	Establish handhold support for dalit leaders	Elected dalit representatives federation has been created and it was assisted by the chair.	Entire state
12.	Establish handhold support for local body leaders	One local body supplement in a newspaper was published for one year	For the whole state

Source: Rajiv Gandhi Chair, "Ten Years of Activities on Decentralization of Powers", Gandhigram: Rajiv Gandhi Chair for Panchayati Raj Studies, 2014.

Conclusion

What was aimed at India through the 73rd Amendment to the Constitution of India is to decentralize powers to local bodies through a process of democratization. Decentralization has to happen through democratic means and that is why it is called democratic decentralization. Even the representative democratic institutions are struggling to keep the democratic values in the attitude and behaviour of the people who are involved in decision-making. One has to wonder how it will happen at the community level where all antithetical practices to democratic values are in operation. To make it happen, a sufficient condition has to be created for democratization while decentralizing powers. Mere enactment of the Act is only a necessary condition but putting the necessary wherewithal will create a sufficient condition for effective decentralization.

Hence, democratization is as important as decentralization. Both have potentials. Both are complementary to each other. Necessary conditions have been created by both Central government and state governments. Sufficient conditions have to be created by the civil society organisations, media, training institutions and the intellectuals. For democracy promotion, ground rules creation and effective implementation could be done only by the higher level learning institutions. Social science departments in higher learning institutions can facilitate democracy promotional activities. To demonstrate how it could be done, I have explained the activities of the Rajiv Gandhi Chair for Panchayati Raj Studies in Gandhigram Rural Institute in the area of democratic decentralization of powers. It requires only passion not a mandate from anybody.

Notes and References

1. Myron Weiner (1989), "Indian Paradoxes", New Delhi: Sage Publications.
2. Rajendra Vova and Suhas Palshikar (eds.) (2004), "Indian Democracy: Meanings and Practices", New Delhi: Sage Publications.
3. Peter Mair (2008), "Democracies" in Daniel Caramani (ed.), 'Comparative Politics', New York: Oxford University Press.
4. Paul Ginsborg (2009), "Democracy Crisis and Renewal", London: Profile Books.
5. Jean Baechler (1998), "Democracy: An Analytical Survey", New Delhi: National Book Trust India.

6. M.K. Gandhi (1960), "Hind Swaraj", Ahmedabad: Navjeevan Publications.
7. James Manor (2010), "Local Governance" in Niraja Gopal Jayal and Pratap Bhanu Mehta (eds.), 'The Oxford Companion to Politics in India', New Delhi: Oxford University Press.
8. James Manor (1999), "The Political Economy of Decentralization", Washington D.C.: The World Bank.
9. Rajni Kothari (2005), "Rethinking Democracy", New Delhi: Orient Longman.
10. Arend Lijphart (1982), "Democracy in Plural Societies: A Comparative Explanation", Bombay: Popular Prakashan.
11. Jayaprakash Narayan (1964), Presidential Address in the Fourth National All India Panchayat Parishad Conference held in Bangalore on July 18.
12. Barbara Geddes (2007), "What Causes Democratization?" in Carles Boix and Susan C. Stokes (eds), 'The Oxford Hand Book of Comparative Politics', New York: Oxford University Press.
13. Robert A. Dahl (1972), "Authority in a Good Society", New Delhi: Allied Publishers.
14. Peter Burnell (2008), "Promoting Democracy" in Daniel Caramani (ed.), 'Comparative Politics', New York: Oxford University Press.
15. Jacques Thomassen (2009), "Democratic Values" in Russel J. Dalton and Hans-Dieter Klingemann (eds.), 'The Oxford Hand Book of Political Behaviour', New York: Oxford University Press.

2

Democracy and Inequality: A Study of Muslims in India

Mirza Asmer Beg

Section I

The rise of nation-states in Europe encouraged mono-cultural societies. The policies of these nation-states ensured that members of minority communities got a step-motherly treatment. Minorities were expected to conventionally follow the national culture, which was not necessarily consonant with their cultural approach. But India was a different type of nation-state, which dared to experiment with a truly multicultural society. It led to the issue of minorities and their rights coming into sharp focus. However, since Independence, national policies on language, education and other cultural themes have led to the downgrading and break-up of minority culture. Given these conditions, particular community rights are needed both for counteracting the existing form of marginalization faced by minorities in the nation-state, and for protecting minority distinctiveness?

At the theoretical level, where democracy is defined as one in which everyone has a share, it may secure the rights of all the components of the society. However in the modern times, in which representative democracy is in fashion, democracy at the operational level is more and more recognized with majority rule. An essential reason for minority rights is the misleading notion that democracy can defend the interests of minority groups. In its unadulterated variety, however, where it is defined as one in which everyone has a share, democracy may guarantee the rights of all the constituents of the society.

Minority communities living in a democratic polity like India, experience situations of extreme hurt and loss when they realise that their traditions are of modest worth, and that they should assimilate into the dominant practice. This open assertion of majoritarian power unavoidably leads to a politically charged situation, and minorities consequently tend to organize. As they have no resource other than cultural self-sufficiency, or the right to protect their uniqueness in the face of such assertions. The politics of incorporation, therefore, gives rise to heightened political tensions. It is the aggressive and often coercive assimilation of minorities that has led to the sharp drawing of community frontiers.

Minorities exist in all modern nation-states and their typical issues present challenges before all the societies. Towards this end, the policies and institutional responses are worked out. The process of reaching out to the minorities and their ensuing integration into mainstream polity and society is a slow and incremental process. Members of a minority community often experience devaluation and marginalization collectively, and it is because of this, that they need collective protective safeguards in the form of minority rights.

Since Independence in 1947, the Congress party, which has been in power for most of the time, adopted a policy of protection towards the minorities. Apart from the Constitutional safeguards, the secular ideology of the leaders like Nehru also helped the minorities in having a feeling of security, if not a rightful space in the public sphere. The rightist forces which wanted to see India as a Hindu state were kept at a distance, and minorities were treated as equal citizens. They were given equal rights in the Constitution and special provisions were made for the protection of educational and cultural rights of the minorities.

However, while the weaker sections got precise economic benefits, the minorities, particularly the Muslims, were to be satisfied only with the assurances of their security and protection of their personal laws. Consequently, the scheme which dominated the Congress design for Muslims was to steer clear of their real issues and periodically play up emotive issues to give them an impression that the party was quite concerned about their welfare. Even this lip-service to Muslim concerns, was not palatable to the rightist parties, and they continued with their propaganda of Muslim appeasement. Even the setting up of the Prime Minister's High Powered Committee, popularly called the Sachar Committee, was called an appeasement.

In view of the apathy on the part of successive governments and the lack of any concerted efforts for uplift, even on the part of Muslims, the community continued to go down the abyss. Against the backdrop of the prevailing conditions of the Muslims of India, we need to ponder over the possible remedial measures, which if taken, can lead to ameliorating the conditions of the Muslims and take India ahead towards the path of nation-building.

Muslims in India are faced with multiple problems and therefore there is a need for devising a multi pronged approach to involve them in the process of nation-building. Presently, they find themselves in a tight corner with very little room for manoeuvrability. But a basic failure of the community in general has been their inability to define their problems in concrete terms and to think of effective methodologies to tackle these problems. In view of the failure of the Muslims to define their problems and to shape their agenda, this has been done by 'others'. Usually, it has been the Government which has performed this task. Their agenda has been set by the successive Governments, ably assisted by the media and other forces inimical to them, and Muslims have only responded to this thoughtlessly.

Not only were the problems of Muslims defined by the Government, but it also prescribed remedies. Whether the definition was proper or not, or the prescriptions were useful or not, the government was least concerned. The Muslim community never tried to intervene in this discourse. It never acted on its own. It only reacted to what was presented before it as 'the Muslim issue'. Although, Muslims were the rightful stakeholders in this exercise, but no effort was made to involve them in this process, nor did they make any concerted effort to enter into this process. In view of the all too evident apathy and insensitivity of Governments, their real problems have never figured on the agenda, and their response has usually been reactive to issues, which have time and again been thrust upon them.

In view of several governmental reports available today, there is no scarcity of evidence in the public sphere, of the all too evident backwardness of the Muslims of India. The State machinery too, after long years of dilly-dallying, has apparently come to the general understanding that something needs to be done as regards the existential problems of Muslims, who constitute about 14 percent of the Indian population and but for their uplift, one cannot think of the development of the country.

Over the years, some initiatives have been taken by the government, but one fundamental reason why a number of these well-advertised schemes have not yielded the desired results, has been the appallingly low budgetary allocation for programmes directed at socio-economic development of this disadvantaged community.

The per capita Plan allocation for minorities in 2014-15 was as low as ₹ 149, as against the national per capita budgetary outlay of ₹ 14,220. The allocations of ₹ 3,738 crore for Ministry of Minority Affairs (MoMA) include ₹ 3,713 crore under plan and ₹ 25 crore under non-plan. The allocations comprise ₹ 3,618 crore under revenue section and ₹ 120 crore under the capital section. The meagre allocations for the MoMA, work out to less than 0.21 percent of India's total budgetary expenditure of ₹ 17,77,477 crore projected for the ensuing financial year. On the other hand, allocations made include ₹ 30,851 crore for SCs, ₹ 19,980 crore for STs and ₹ 79,258 crore for women.

Against this backdrop, it seems important that Muslim intellectuals should take the lead in articulating the rightful grievances of the community, and communicating them to the government in the form of implementable proposals. And more importantly, then following them up, to see the extent to which they actually benefit the community.

Monitoring the implementation of government initiatives for Muslims is important, because we have seen in the past that most schemes earmarked for minorities in India, have remained only on paper, and the real beneficiaries have been almost insignificant.

Another problem has been that over these years, generally when the government has implemented programmes to uplift the depressed sections of the Indian society, it has conveniently left the Muslims out of it. In 1950, when the Government initiated an affirmative action plan to uplift dalits, it excluded Muslim dalits.

In 1989, when the Government initiated the Mandal Commission affirmative action plan for the OBCs, it again left out the Muslim OBCs. With about half of the Indian Muslims belonging to either SC or OBC category, such exclusion from affirmative action plans has caused further deterioration in the educational and socio-economic status of the Muslim community.

Some of the initiatives, directed at the Muslims, manage to get support from the State, but as there is weak central coordination, the impact of these efforts does not reach the desired level. To empower the Muslims, it is essential to equip them, to help themselves. Muslims must be assisted by the government to set up their educational and financial institutions in a planned manner, and for this to be fruitful, we need to set up a National Consultancy Centre for Muslims. Such a centre would coordinate all welfare activities, where the NGOs, community leaders and the Government would be the main actors (Beg, 2102: 35).

Section II

Some initiatives if taken in the right earnest can go a long way in helping the Muslim community. A major positive intervention in tackling the question of poverty of Muslims of India can be made by the development of Wakf properties. India has around four lakh acres of Wakf land, half of which has been encroached upon or is under dispute. Even if the remaining half is properly developed, there would be no dearth of finances for welfare of Muslims.

The Ministry of Minority Affairs needs to take up this issue and prepare a plan for Wakf development. An institutional structure needs to be put in place to develop Wakf properties. We already have a Joint Parliamentary Committee Report on Wakf, but no subsequent Action taken Report has been presented, which shows the callousness and apathy as regards this serious issue.

The JPC Report says that if ₹ 10,000 crore are invested for developing the Wakf properties, the Muslim community can have an yearly income of ₹ 10,000 crore. Hence, we need to structure a Wakf Development Corporation, with a dispute redressal forum, at the national level (Beg, 2012: 34).

There is a need for a proper understanding of the concepts of nationalism and national integration, which earlier had very positive implications in our society and they were understood in inclusivist terms. However, they have slowly come to acquire negative and exclusivist connotations. We need to redefine these concepts in human rights perspective.

Under the international human rights standards, inclusive democratic integration means providing *de facto* equality to under-represented minorities by special measures, so that all national institutions in the common public domain become socially diverse with effective representation of minorities. It is by sharing the public space in schools/colleges, the work place, the residential areas, the market and decision-making forums and legislatures that communities get integrated.

The Government of India needs to implement the

directions of the Supreme Court (September 2006) for reorganization of the police on the model suggested by the National Police Commission (1979-81), provided for in the Model Police Act, 2006, especially the direction for constituting: (i) Central/State Security Commission/Board, (ii) Police Establishment Board, (iii) Police Complaints Authority/Accountability Commission (The other reform measures like separation of the investigation and law and order functions may be implemented at a later stage, if the excuse of insufficient number of police personnel is found to be genuine) and (iv) Provision of adequate minority representation in all wings of the police, as recommended by the NPC and other commissions and committees as well as by the Sorabjee Model Police Drafting Committee (2006).

There is a crying need to empower the National Commission on Human Rights to carry out its mandate of protection and promotion of human rights, especially right to equality and non-discrimination, more proactively and effectively, for which the existing National Commissions on religious minorities, linguistic minorities, women, SC and ST and children, disabled and for any other identified disadvantaged group, may function as sub-commissions for the purposes of ensuring equal opportunities/non-discrimination to the concerned groups.

It will require suitable amendment of the Protection of Human Rights Act, 1993, though even under the existing provisions of clause 12(d), (f) and (g) it can perform all the functions defined in the Model Act of the Equal Opportunities Commission.

When under the shadow of Partition draft constitution, provision for population based quota for minorities in legislatures was scrapped in May 1949; firm assurance was given to them that they would get more than their fair share in Parliament, assemblies and the cabinet.

However, since 1952, Muslim representation in Lok Sabha and Assemblies has been about 50 percent of their expected share, which has been noted by the National Commission to

Review the Working of the Constitution as well as by the Sachar Committee, which have recommended the presence of effective Muslim voice in all bodies. Their representation touched a new low in 2014.

It, therefore, requires introducing measures in the electoral system providing for effective representation of Muslims and other underrepresented minorities in legislatures and other elected bodies and decision-making forums. This neglected issue raised by NCRWC and more forcefully by Sachar Committee needs special attention.

The exercise for the delimitation of constituencies needs to offer opportunity for all those social groups which feel their representation in the legislatures does not reflect their numerical strength, which is the very essence of democracy and socio-political justice. It has been observed that often constituencies with large percentage of Muslims are reserved for the SCs.

The Sachar Committee (2006) also took a serious note of the way constituencies with a sufficiently large number of Muslims were reserved for SCs. Other structural reforms on the lines of systems in place in some European countries may also be considered.

For Muslims, security has always been a major issue. Muslims have all these years reconciled to living as second class citizens, provided their security is ensured. Thousands of communal riots since Independence have created such a fear psychosis among Muslims that they have not only shrunk in their physical ghettoes, in cities and town, but their thinking has also been affected by this existential condition.

The concern for security has been uppermost in their minds, and once it is taken care of, they are satisfied and do not care to demand their rightful share in the national cake. Many a governments have taken advantage of this fear in the 'Muslim Mind', by not doing anything substantial for them, except for giving them physical security, and getting their votes.

Hence, Muslims have actually been viewed by political parties only as vote banks, whose votes can be garnered by playing with the ever lurking fear of security in their minds. The basic reason for this fear is the conduct of police and paramilitary forces in situations of communal conflict. Several commissions of enquiry set-up by the government have clearly indicted the local administration and police force for partiality and high-handedness.

To instil confidence among the Muslims and to give them a sense of security, we suggest that a multi-religious police force academy be set up, which would be entrusted with the task of recruiting and training police personnel for multi-religious backgrounds. The composition of this police force would resemble the diverse nature of the society.

In a communally charged situation, a policeman should perceive of the community, which he is policing, as an ally and not as an enemy. What creates the biggest fear among the minority community, in such a situation, is a biased police force. We suggest that in a situation like this, the multi-religious police force, (like they have in Switzerland and Macedonia) which polices a Muslim majority area, should have a majority of Muslims. A multi-religious police force was also suggested by the Sorabjee Model Police Drafting Committee (2006).

Their exercise of authority should be regulated by defined procedures, and any misuse should be subject to the severest punishment. Nothing can generate more confidence and dispel the fear among Muslims, than the understanding that the police force which has been deployed for their security would at least try to come true to its mandate and it does not view them as enemies. We need to have quotas in the police force for different religious groups.

We also need to have a National Unity Department, which would oversee the efforts towards confidence building of the minorities. It is also essential to establish a statutory National/State Community Relations Commission (CRC) for monitoring and resolution of inter-community/group conflicts especially on ethno-religious issues as recommended by the NCM Report, 1999 (Beg, 2102: 36).

Frequently, we have seen that inquiries by official Commissions and NGOs have revealed the fact that all these acts of mass hate violence have been successfully carried out by the complicity of the State's agencies, especially the partisan role of the police under direction or lack of direction from the political executive.

Such complicity has been testified by senior civil servants and police officers. The justice system in India has not only not come to the rescue of the victims, its own functioning establishes a pattern of neglect and bias which has encouraged a insidious climate of impunity, which is a source of reappearance of violence.

Lack of any law on the rights of victims, leaves those who have suffered losses of life, limb, property and livelihood to depend on the mercy of the same political executive for relief, rehabilitation and compensation, whose complicity has been the cause of their suffering.

Except for cases like that of victims of 1984 anti-Sikh carnage, the judiciary has not done justice to victims by directing the governments to uniformly apply the same standards for compensation and rehabilitation of all victims irrespective of faith. A good example of how State terrorizes citizens and communities, especially Muslims, is provided by the Hashmipura (Meerut) case wherein hundreds of Muslims were picked up from their houses on May 22, 1987, out of which 42 young Muslims were shot dead by PAC personnel and their bodies were thrown into the upper Ganga canal and Hindon river in Ghaziabad District. The CBCID of UP took seven years to complete and submit the inquiry report of the incident in which these facts were confirmed.

The Government of U.P. filed charges only against 19 PAC personnel—all of lower rank, in the court of CJM Ghaziabad in May 1996. However, all those 19 accused charged with conspiracy, murder, and attempt to murder and concealment of facts, continued to be in active service and lived as free citizens even after 1996 charge sheet. The successive Governments of U.P. never produced them before the CJM Ghaziabad's Court. After great public pressure, they surrendered in June-July 2000, and were easily granted bail.

Eventually, a Delhi court in March 2015, acquitted all 16 accused citing insufficient evidence. A counsel for the victims and survivors, Rebecca John summed it, "If today is not the day we hang our heads in shame, there can be no other day", she said after the verdict (The Times of India, 2015). The next of kin of the forty two persons killed were given only ₹ 40,000 in 1987.

All efforts of seeking adequate compensation generally paid in such cases, from the judiciary as well as the political executive failed. More than 2,000 people were killed in Nellie in Assam in 1983, not one single person was eventually convicted for this pogrom. 900 people died in Bombay riots of 1993. Only three convictions took place in those riot cases (The Telegraph, 2015). The conviction rate in the Gujarat riots (2002) has been the worst so far, a negligible between 0.21 and 1.18 percent (Stanford Law School, Gujarat Riots Report: 2014).

Effective protection needs to be provided to minority languages and other areas of minority culture and religion, which require stronger protection, especially when inter-community relations are not cordial.

The unproductive debate over Uniform Civil Code conceived of in secular-communal discourse needs to come to an end in the wake of acceptance of human rights norm of multiculturalism, requiring pluralism of family laws, provided no traditional community based law is violative of human rights of members, especially women and children. It is, therefore, required to amend the Constitution giving protection to community-based family laws, provided they are not inconsistent with human rights standards.

Some sections among Muslims complain that their share in

Government jobs is low because of the discriminatory attitude of the recruiting bodies. Although it is difficult to empirically substantiate these charges, but if we look at the representation of Muslims in category C and D jobs, where the requirements of educational qualifications are minimal or non-existent, one is forced to consider the discrimination thesis seriously.

Provisions need to be made for better representation of Muslims in jobs where their lack of educational qualification is not a handicap for them. Diversity in organizations needs to be incentivized. People need to be educated about the advantages of diversity.

Equitable justice is indispensable for a balanced growth of our country. The first step towards secular justice, which is the bare minimum requirement of any secular state, would be for the Government to publish: (a) all information about ex-gratia compensation/relief paid to all sufferers of disturbances at least since 1980-81; (b) all information on riot related cases filed, investigation/prosecution and conviction or cases dismissed/withdrawn with reasons of dismissal and withdrawal since 1980-81; (c) all information on targeted killings/ encounter killings of Muslims and custodial crimes against them with hate motive; and (d) all information on detainees under counter-terror operations. This is important to counter all kinds of canards and distortions which shape our perception and thinking (Beg, 2012: 39).

Section III

As the problems are complex and deep-rooted, we do not intend to give some quick and easy solutions. It is going to be a long-term national enterprise. We have to bring in workable policies and also build bridges of goodwill and understanding across India.

We need to appreciate and make every Indian understand that the problems of Muslims in India are not the problems of this community alone, they are problems of the Indian nation, and they have to be tackled as challenges by all of us. It is the government's basic responsibility to assist the destitute Muslim community out of poverty and exclusion. With a new government in place in Delhi in 2014, many in the community were apprehensive, but some voices have expressed hope. Sabir Ali JD (U) Rajya Sabha M.P. said the new government must be given an opportunity to ensure welfare of the Muslim community. "Let us come out of past, join hands to strengthen the government led by PM Modiji", (TOI, 2014) he said, hitting at previous Congress governments for exploiting Muslims as a vote bank.

However, the present government scores better than the UPA on several counts. Like the scheme, *Nai Roshini*, which was launched with much fanfare by the UPA in January 2010, the Ministry of Minority Affairs did not spend a single rupee till 2012-13, when ₹ 10 crore were spent and a total of 36,950 women benefited under it.

In stark contrast, Minister of Minority Affairs in the NDA, facilitated the empowerment of 68,675 women at a cost of ₹ 13.48 crore under the same scheme during 2014-15. For digitising the Wakf Board records, the UPA spent ₹ 89 lakh during 2012-13 against the revised estimate of ₹ 1.65 crore and ₹ 2.98 crore against the revised estimate of ₹ 3 crore in 2013-14.

On the other hand, the NDA Government spent the entire allocated amount of ₹ 3 crore during 2014-15. The UPA in 2013-14, had spent a meagre ₹ 1.91 crore from the allocated ₹ 7 crore on strengthening of State Wakf Boards. The NDA spent ₹ 3.95 crore against the revised estimate of ₹ 4 crore in 2014-15 for the same.

Hence, contrary to popular perceptions, the present government would not fare too badly when compared to the previous one in terms of what it has done for the minorities. However, it has been only about three years since the new government has assumed office, and it is too short a period to reach to any conclusion about its performance vis-à-vis the minorities, especially the Muslims of India.

References

Beg, Mirza Asmer and A.R. Kidwai (2012) (eds.), "Muslims in India: An Action Plan in Empowerment of Indian Muslims: Perspectives, Planning and Road Ahead", Concept Publishing Company, New Delhi,

Stanford Law School (2014), "Gujarat Riots Report", May.

The Times of India, December 31, 2014.

The Times of India, March 22, 2015.

The Telegraph, July 30, 2015.

3

State, Globalization and Agrarian Situation

J. Prabhash and A. Mohanakumar

The impact of economic globalisation on agriculture and allied sectors is a widely debated issue. There is rich literature in the field which argues that it plays a significant role in the decline of agriculture and deepening the crisis in the sector. This is not merely in terms of removing protectionism and trade barriers which used to quarantine the agricultural economy from exposure to competition from abroad. While all these are really important, the crucial issue is the change in the very nature of the state, its antipathy towards the primary sector which borders on indifference and callousness, its craze for economic growth and the gross paternalism it shows towards the secondary and tertiary sectors.

Today, it works in a manner as if it takes into reckoning only the market forces and the 'economic growth' these forces are supposed to generate. All other concerns which matter people the most, from basic survival needs to environmental issues, seem to be of little consequence for it. Therefore, what matters for the state now is the production of things rather than production of relationships that provide agency to the people (Patnaik, 2014: 5).

This definitely marks the movement from the preambular pledge of the Indian Constitution to ensure social justice to the people to the WTO prescriptions which seek to ensure 'market justice'. The agrarian situation in India has to be situated against this context.

That agricultural activities need state support in adequate measure is a long settled proposition. This is not only because of the salient role it plays in the development of other sectors—especially the secondary sector—but also since in an agrarian economy land is the crucial means of survival for vast majority of the population. An important area like this, therefore, could not be left to the forays of private parties who eye on maximising returns with minimum of investment. Public intervention and investment, thus, assume centrality (Chakravarthy, 1993; Feder et al., 1985; Patnaik, 2007; Shyjan, 2007).

Needless to say, such interventions may take different forms like providing research and support services, development of physical infrastructure, credit market support, increasing productivity, provision against market failure etc. In India, for instance, the presence of the state has been visible in almost every spher. in the agricultural sector ranging from controlling the prices in the factor market (fertilizers, pesticides, water and minimum wages) to product market and in the form of intervention in other areas (Deshpande and Arora, 2012: 10).

It is this long history of state intervention that economic globalisation has been doing away with since the last two and a half decades. As part of trade liberalisation in agriculture, the state has to fulfil certain commitments relating to market access, conditions on domestic support, export subsidies, agreement on intellectual property rights and sanitary and phytosanitary measures (Gulati, 2001: 43). And cumulatively all these meant the following: reduction of domestic subsidies; market access to commodities from abroad; deregulation on domestic manufacturing of fertilizers and liberalising their imports; dismantling food security system; removal of controls on markets, traders and processors and subsidies to cooperatives; abolition of Essential Commodities Act and inventory controls; abolition of selective credit control on investment and finance; treating farmers' cooperatives on an equal footing with the private sector; and moving agriculture in the direction of enhancing self-regenerative ecological process and enhancing ecological and livelihood security (Iyer,

2005: 62; Adiseshiah, 1994: 6).

On the basis of this, Reddy and Mishra (2012: 55 and 58) argue: Economic reforms agenda extensively destabilised livelihoods of small and marginal farmers. Over the years, the rising costs, volatile commodity prices and dwindling public investment in agriculture (have) caused a great deal of vulnerability in the livelihood of the farming community. Further, there has been an increasing pressure on the farmers in terms of meeting basic social services like education and health, which are increasingly privatized and are becoming a considerable part of domestic expenditure needs.

The state, thus, rolled itself back from intervention in human affairs and rolled out a set of policies which are carried out not on behalf of the common good, but rather on behalf of the globalisation project (Munck, 2005: 63; Harvey, 2007: 66). The argument here is not that liberalization *per se* is responsible for the agrarian distress, though it is definitely one of the primary reasons for it. It is against this background that the agrarian situation in Kerala has to be discussed. This paper analyses the problem in the specific context of the middle class farmers in Kottayam district. [1] The paper is divided into two sections. The first section deals with certain specificities of Kerala's agricultural scenario and how globalisation has impacted on it; and the second part discusses the empirical findings.

Specificities of Kerala Agriculture and the Impact of Economic Globalisation

The agrarian situation in Kerala is noted for certain features which are peculiar to the state. The number of households whose principal occupation is agriculture is only 22 percent as against the national average of 57.8 percent, and even here only 16 percent have declared cultivation as the main source of income (GoK, 2015: 39). The state is also noted for highly fragmented nature of land holdings, shortage of labour supply and high degree of commercialisation of agriculture.

According to available statistics, there are 68.31 lakh operational land holdings possessing 15.11 lakh hectares with an average size of 0.22 hectare (Table 3.1). The table shows that in 96.33 percent of cases, land holding is less than one hectare. This actually shows the extent to which Kerala agriculture is characterized by atomization of land. On the other side, a structural transformation has also been taking place in Kerala as land used for food grain crops came down drastically in the face of increasing commercialisation of agriculture and putting land to non-agricultural uses.

Table 3.1: Number of Operational Holdings and Area Operated by Size Class: 2010-2011

Size of holding (hectare)	Number in '000	Percentage	Area (in '000 hectares)
Below 1.00	6,580	96.33	886
1.00-1.99	180	2.64	282
2.00-3.99	57	0.83	159
4.00-9.99	12	0.18	64
10.00 and above	2	0.02	120
Total	6,831	100	1,511

Source: Government of Kerala, *Economic Review, Volume II*, Trivandrum: Planning Board, 2015, p. 44.

While many reasons were pointed for this—calculation of the farmers in terms of maximisation of income (Oomman, 1963), increase in wage rate, and ill conceived development (Kannan and Pushpangadan, 1998: A120), exemption of plantation crops from Land Reforms Act, and the promotional activities of the central and state governments in favour of cash crops (Pillai, 1994: 60)—encouragement given by the World Bank in the cultivation of export earning crops like coconut, pepper, cashew, coca and spices through what is known as Kerala Agricultural Development Project merits serious consideration (Andrews, 2013: 21).

As a result, of the gross cropped area of 26.1 lakh hectares in 2013-14, only 10.32 percent was put to food crop cultivation whereas the same was 60 percent for cash crops (GoK, 2015: 41 and 45). Further, just four crops—rubber, tea, coffee and cardamom—occupy about 45 percent of the land used for growing cash crops. All these show that the cropping pattern which gradually developed in the state is such that it always remained linked with the requirements of the global market.

Shortage of labour and incidence of high wage rate are the other two prominent aspects of the agricultural economy of Kerala. Labour shortage is a consequence of labour migration to other sectors of the economy and could be traced back to the land reforms period which, *inter alia,* paved the way for the liberation of the toiling classes who until then were tied to the land as part of the feudal system. Interestingly, this movement of labour which was initially inter-sectoral in nature slowly changed and became inter-state and even international. Recall the Keralites' strong presence in other parts of India and also in the Gulf countries. An important side effect of this is the increase in real wages for agricultural workers (Baby, 1996) as well as the rise in prices of non-tradable inputs including land [2] (Balakrishnan, 1999: 1270).

All the above combined in varying degrees made agriculture—food crop cultivation in particular—unattractive, though the real estate value of the land increased. This is an interesting development which in turn came to have serious implications for agriculture also. It may be recalled that the spurt in migration remittances and the boom in the construction sector (both are related) not only encouraged the use of land for non-agricultural purposes, but also raised its value phenomenally. Harilal and Eswaran (2015: 9) put this in a clear perspective:

This played a major role in boosting the asset function of land at the expense of its means of production function. Migrants, and for that matter anybody with investible funds, consider land as an alternative and at the same time, fairly secure asset for investment. It becomes a self-fulfilling proposition because the flow of remittances into the land market pushes up land prices making it more attractive in terms of capital appreciation...In the context of Kerala, the conversion of land into a speculative asset has assumed alarming proportions and it has become a hindrance to industrial investment too.

This means that Kerala is in a catch 22 situation. Farmers neither cultivate land for fear of incurring loss, nor alienate it except when they are in dire strait, because of its speculative value. This combined with other factors has made Kerala agriculture vulnerable in many respects. It is in a context like this that economic globalisation was introduced.

Interestingly, when strong doses of globalisation policies were introduced during the early nineties, the widely held belief in Kerala was that they would not adversely affect the state and, on the contrary, would even prove beneficial to it given the peculiar characteristics of the state economy and the agrarian sector such as: increased flow of foreign remittances, comparatively low rate of agriculture dependent population and contribution of agriculture to state domestic product, and the strong presence of export oriented cash crops. While all these were sound in theory, in actual practice many of them proved to be the Achilles heel of the state. On the whole, globalisation policies accelerated the process of the decline of the agricultural sector. For instance, its contribution to GSDP declined from 36.88 percent in 1980-81 to a mere 8.95 percent in 2013-14 and its growth performance slid from 1.8 percent in the Tenth Plan to -1.3 percent in the Eleventh Plan and further down to -1.36 percent in 2013-14 (GoK, 2015: 37).

With globalisation policies in full swing, agricultural situation moved from decline to distress. Though hard hit were the food grains cultivators, the crisis slowly engulfed the cash crop cultivators too. Two contradictory pulls became visible in Kerala as in the rest of the country—export of agriculture commodities declined; and import increased with fall in domestic prices of commodities and rise in price volatility (Nair and Maneesh, 2015: 7). Natural rubber is a clear case in point here. The import of the commodity increased from 17,884 MT in 1992-93 to as high as 3,25,190 MT in 2013-14 and during the same period the import of synthetic rubber moved from 47,362 MT to 3,71,839 MT (GoI, 2015: 49). This is so with every other crop including pepper, cashew, tea and coconut. Production of many of these crops also stagnated or registered a steep fall during this time. In a single year (2013-14), decline in production of rubber was to the tune of 9.13 lakh tonnes, pepper 10,000 tonnes, coffee 1530 MT, and cashew 4,544 MT.

Significantly, commodities imported from abroad were done at a price which was lower than that of its prices in Kerala. This was especially so with regard to the commodities imported from Sri Lanka (as part of India-Sri Lanka Free Trade Agreement, 1999) and from the ASEAN countries (as part of India-ASEAN Agreement, 2009). As stated earlier, the commodities thus imported—rubber, coconut, tea, pepper, spices, coffee, and cashew—were the ones in which Kerala had a better track record of production and in some of them like spices and pepper even near monopolistic control. All these also meant integration of domestic prices of these commodities with international prices (Lathika, 2009: 96). Added to this was the rise in the cost of cultivation and decline in product prices. Price parity index prepared by the State Planning Board clearly brings out this phenomenon. According to Table 3.2, for the decennial from 2004 to 2014, the index of prices received by the farmers moved from ₹ 2,651 to ₹ 8,189 only, whereas the index of price paid by them moved from ₹ 4,459 to ₹ 11,294 and the index of cultivation cost moved from ₹ 7,360 to ₹ 22,041.

At the same time, the dominance of perennial crops which implied certain rigidities in the land use pattern made it difficult for farmers to respond immediately to changes in market conditions through adjustments in cropping pattern and to make long-term investment decisions (George, 2005: 2-3), though they resorted to crop shifting widely. And this shift was mainly from food crops to cash crops and also from agricultural purpose to non-agricultural purposes. For example, while the gross cropped area of food crops declined from 37.46 percent in 1980-81 to 10.30 percent in 2012-13, the share of cash crops moved from 44.59 percent to 62.5 percent during the same period (GoK, 2013: 25). And the land put to non-agricultural purposes almost doubled from 2,05,500 hectare in 1960-61 to 4,09,000 hectare in 2004-05 (Lathika, 2009: 110).

Table 3.2: Yearly Average Index Number of Prices Received and Prices Paid by Farmers

Year	Index of prices received by farmers	Index of farm cultivation cost (₹)	Index of domestic expenditure	Index of price paid by farmers	Parity index as Col.2 to 5
2004	2,651	7,360	2,701	4,459	59.00
2005	2,440	7,703	2,795	4,640	53.00
2006	2,474	8,309	2,947	4,947	50.00
2007	2,746	9,135	3,061	5,288	52.00
2008	3,167	10,036	3,394	5,837	54.00
2009	3,083	11,468	3,640	6,460	48.00
2010	3,727	12,824	3,970	7,135	52.00
2011	5,117	14,959	4,398	8,109	63.00
2012	4,743	17,447	4,715	9,070	52.00
2013	6,008	20,422	5,376	10,478	57.08
2014	8,188	22,041	5,787	11,293	72.57

Source: Government of Kerala, *Economic Review, Volume II*, Trivandrum: Planning Board, 2015, p. 30.

Thus, under the weight of economic globalisation, Kerala farmers—middle class in particular—became more and more pauperized. Production of all major crops slumped and their prices tumbled down. While cost of cultivation spiralled, export of agricultural commodities declined and import increased. So was the debt burden of the farming community. Atomization of land also proved to be another burden which put farmers into a disadvantageous position vis-à-vis monopolies and monopolistic players in the market as they could not aggregate their strength through collective action (Hrilal and Eswaran, 2015: 42). Reduction of subsidies by the state, and fall in other support services offered by it made the situation worse. This sums up the impact of economic globalisation on Kerala's agriculture.

The empirical study conducted by the researchers more or less corroborates the discussion made so far. No doubt, economic globalisation is playing havoc with agriculture. This is definitely so in the case of middle class farmers and especially those among them who are engaged in food grain cultivation (GoK, 2015). In our study, 95 percent of the respondents who belonged to this category were not at all satisfied with their vocation as farmers. Though this is only 29 percent for cash crop growers, they also shared their counterparts' (food grain cultivators) desire to quit farming. A total of 319 respondents (79 percent) out of 400, envisaged such a future for them. However, the most important problem for them was to find out a viable alternative to farming. With an average age of around 50 (48.9 to be exact) and with hardly any expertise outside of agriculture, none of the respondents believed that this could be materialized. They are, thus caught between a future which is bleak and a present which is precarious. Therefore, their continuance in farming itself is an ordeal, a kind of tormentation, and an affront to their self-respect as citizens.

The problems the respondents confront as middle class farmers could not be reduced to a mere cost-benefit analysis, income and expenditure, profit and loss—though it is definitely important. The magnitude of the crisis has reached such a proportion to threaten their very life situation—education of their children, marriage of daughters, health and other livelihood concerns of the family, and their general social esteem. As could be conjectured, the core issues they confront in their profession are: fall in production and decline in the price of products, enhanced cost of cultivation, callous attitude of the state and political parties towards farmers' issues and import of cheap products from abroad affecting the market of indigenous commodities.

Fall in Production and Prices of Commodities

An aggregate of 63 percent of the respondents in the study reported a fall/stagnation in productivity irrespective of the nature of the crops cultivated. Though they could not give the exact quantity of such decline and again though there was a tendency for them to overstate the issue, it could be safely concluded that it was anything between 5 to 10 percent from the previous year with intensity being higher for food crops; the decline of which is reported to be over 15 percent. While natural calamities, crop loss due to various diseases and attack by pests were the major reasons pointed out by the respondents, one could also notice that a general lack of interest among them, particularly food grain growers, in cultivation.

For instance, 71.5 percent of the respondents testified to attempts made by them to reduce the cost of cultivation by slashing the use of fertilizers, both chemical and organic, and labour. Interestingly, such practices were resorted to mainly by lower middle class farmers than the rest. Also many of the respondents belonging to all income brackets confessed to the researchers that their enthusiasm for cultivation had been on the wane. While during earlier times even in the midst of crop failures they remained wedded to their vocation and pursued it more vigorously, today all these have given place to despair and hopelessness as the future seems to hold little promise. With help coming from no quarters in desired measures, they feel let down by the state and political parties and also in low spirit, they say. All these, no doubt, had affected their interest in agriculture.

The situation is further aggravated by the fall in the prices of agricultural commodities and a simultaneous increase in the cost of cultivation. All the respondents voiced their concern on both the counts. According to them, the gap between income and expenditure was more than three-fold, i.e. for every one rupee earned by the farmer through the sale of crops; he/she had to spend more than three rupees as the cost of inputs. Interestingly, more than the food crop cultivators it is the cash crop farmers who have to face the brunt as price volatility consequent upon trade liberalisation affected them most because of stiff competition from abroad. This is especially so in the case of pepper, rubber, coffee and tea. Among the food grain growers, the situation proved to be grim for paddy cultivators.

While prices fell like this, input cost increased enormously. Price of fertilizers and labour wage are the two instances that merit special consideration here. It may be noted that Kerala is one of the states where the application of chemical fertilizers is the highest especially since the 1980s (Mani, 65). With the increased use of fertilizer also came escalation of their prices, particularly that of factomphos, urea and potassium, and artificial scarcity created by the producers and distributors who have monopoly control over them. According to the respondents, all their attempts at offsetting the cost of cultivation through reduction in fertilizer consumption not only came to a not because of this, but cut in their application also resulted in production fall as mentioned earlier.

Labour also contributed to the vows of the farmers in a two-fold manner: increase in the wage rate and shortage of labour supply. According to an official estimate, average increase in wages (in percentage terms) of male unskilled workers in the agricultural sector for the ten year period from 2004-05 to 2014-15 was 13.03 and that of the female workers was 13.82. Interestingly, this is much higher than the wage rate of even skilled workers like carpenters which increased for the same decennial only by 11.78 percent (GoK, 2015: 31).

Further, the field data shows that the gap between the two is even higher. For, according to the respondents, the actual wage rate of labourers engaged in food crop cultivation ranged from ₹ 500 to ₹ 550 and that of those engaged in plantation crops between ₹ 600 to ₹ 800, taking the percentage increase to as high as 66 and 84, respectively (Mohanakumar, 2013: 148). Apart from this, a minority of the respondents (20.3 percent) also cited shortage of labour as a perennial issue they confronted. In fact, this is a state-wide phenomenon and is a by-product of developments like Gulf boom, better prospects in other sectors and the implementation of projects like Mahatma Gandhi National Rural Employment Guarantee Scheme (Table 3.3).

Table 3.3: Average Daily Wage Rates of Unskilled Workers in the Agricultural Sector

Agricultural Year	Average Daily Wage Rates of Paddy Field Workers (percent increase from previous year)			
	Male		Female	
2004-05	165.58	11.33	115.75	13.9
2005-06	166.39	0.49	108.19	-6.53
2006-07	179.01	7.58	123.96	14.58
2007-08	195.97	9.47	137.42	10.86
2008-09	224.40	14.51	159.02	15.72
2009-10	260.11	15.91	185.40	16.59
2010-11	312.82	20.26	228.48	23.24
2011-12	373.06	14.26	273.19	19.57
2012-13	439.01	17.68	323.67	18.48
2013-14	499.60	13.80	361.67	11.74

Source: Government of Kerala, *Economic Review, Volume II*, Trivandrum: Planning Board, 2015, p. 33.

Exploitation of middlemen and lack of income from non-farm activities have further compounded the situation. Intervention by middlemen is a rampant source of concern raised by the respondents and this takes place in many forms ranging from lending money to encouraging farmers to go for distress sale and procuring farm products at sub-optimal prices. All these are related and have at their core financial support offered by private money lenders who, in most cases, are also middlemen.

It may be recalled that indebtedness of agricultural households is the highest in Kerala. According to the Situation Assessment Survey of Agricultural Households conducted by the NSSO (70th Round, 2013), 77.7 percent of the agricultural households in the state were found to be indebted as against 52 percent at the national level, and the average amount of loan outstanding was a massive, ₹ 2,13,600 as against ₹ 47,000 for the country as a whole (Government of India, 2014). On the other hand, Kerala farmers depend more on institutional credit rather than borrowing money from informal sources like private money lenders.

Our study varies to a certain extent from the above findings. For instance, the percentage of indebted farmers comes only to 62.25 (249) and among them a considerable number—102 (40.96 percent)—borrowed money from private lenders. The total outstanding debt was ₹ 1,89,69,299 with an average of ₹ 76,181.92. The reason cited by the indebted farmers for non-dependence on formal credit sources—commercial banks in particular—makes an interesting reading. Two important among them were: technical and procedural difficulties (39.5 percent) and nominal nature of loan amount available on land mortgage (Mohanakumar, 2013: 182).

There is an element of truth in this contention. It may be remembered that for commercial banks, agricultural lending is the last priority, given the fact that it is a loss making venture and a crisis ridden sector of the economy because of which reimbursement of loan is really problematic. [3] Further, given the fragmented nature of the land holding in the state, the scale of finance which could be made available as loan is very much limited and, additionally, many of the stipulations of the National Bank for Agricultural and Rural Development (NABARD) have little relevance for the Kerala situation.

Another important cause of worry for the respondents (9.4 percent) in this regard is the bank's preference for providing agricultural loans on gold guarantee. And this is a serious issue for the cultivators, who have enough of land but little of gold.

A discussion on the purpose for which the borrowers have spent the money is also in order here. Needless to say, in the literature on agrarian crisis and farmer's indebtedness, there is an important argument that loans are used for non-agricultural purposes rather than for meeting the crisis. This is particularly so in the case of Kerala. The Situation Assessment Survey of Farmers (NSSO, 59th Round), for instance, points out in the specific context of Kerala, that only 21.4 percent of the loan amount was utilized for the purpose for which it was taken as against the national average of 58.4 percent.

Our study presents an interesting picture in this regard. The first impression one gathers from the analysis of the data is that 41.80 percent of the borrowers had used the loan amount for agricultural purposes and the rest (58.19 percent) diverted it on the basis of extraneous considerations. However, looking at the break-up of the expenditure incurred by the former group brings out a different reality—73 percent of them used it for servicing the existing debt and only the rest invested in agriculture. With regard to the latter category, 90.16 percent spent it for meeting household expenditure like education and marriage of their children and the remaining as investment in non-farm business.

A crop-wise analysis of cultivators shows that, among the borrowers, food crop cultivators constitute the majority—61.48 percent and their priority in spending is as follows: 44 percent spent on meeting household expenses, 34.67 percent on servicing existing debt, 16 percent on investing in agriculture and 5 percent on non-farming business. The percentage distribution of cash crop cultivators in this respect is 46.8, 23.4, 4.3 and 22.5, respectively. Thus, it is clear that there is lot of diversion in spending agricultural loan. That said, however, it is doubtful whether one could blame the farmers for this as it is basically due to the force of circumstances rather than a wilful act of defiance. In a situation in which the existing loan has become a drag on their finances and agriculture itself has become a loss making venture, they are forced to divert the loan amount for meeting their daily needs, in most cases against their own wishes.

Viewed thus, borrowing itself has become a coping strategy with the farmers to meet both the agrarian crisis as well as the problems in their personal life. Minimizing family expenses, alienating property, distress sale of agricultural produce, shifting cropping pattern and migrating to other occupations are the other strategies they usually follow. A vast majority of the respondents (60 percent) have testified to curtailing their personal and family expenses including those relating to education, marriage, food, clothing, purchase of consumer durables and even health care wherever possible. Crop-wise, 49 percent of cash crop cultivators and 61 percent of food crop cultivators followed any one or combination of such strategies.

Many of these respondents told the researchers telltale stories of children being shifted from private schools to nearby government schools, delayed marriages or marriages whose expenses were drastically whittled down, and denial of timely medical care to the family members. They seemed to be particularly concerned about the current conjuncture in which they had to depend, *per force*, on the market for everything from schooling to daily consumption needs. We have come across three instances of paddy cultivators who had to depend on open market even for rice as they often went for distress sale of paddy. Again, having placed above the poverty line by the state, they are not eligible for subsidized rice distributed through the PDS as well.

A minority of the respondents (7.5 percent) have attempted at occupational changes without any degree of success. As most of them were ill-trained and ill-suited for vocations outside farming, all of them were forced to turn back to their original profession. At the same time, felling trees and selling them as timber and, in rare cases, alienating landed property were also resorted to by a few (2 percent). On the other hand, 60.5 percent had attested to the widespread occurrence of this phenomenon in their neighbourhood. According to them, this has become rampant in Kottayam district within the span of last ten to fifteen years (Mohanakumar, 2013: 163). Added to this is the tendency for crop shifting. Among our respondents, 31.55 percent (126) had practiced this. As could be conjectured, this was mainly from food crops to cash crops (88.1 percent). Significantly, those who had shifted to cash crops revealed that the strategy proved to be financially rewarding compared to their tryst with food crops.

Distress sale of farm products was also widely practiced. Fifty two percent of the respondents had reported that they indulged in such practices. An interesting observation that could be made here is that this was seen more among middle income farmers than others. For instance, among the 209 respondents who said that they practiced it, 126 (60.3 percent) belonged to this group (monthly income of ₹ 5000-₹ 10,000), and the same is only 13.4 percent among the higher income group (₹ 10,000 and above) and 26.3 percent among the lower income farmers (less than ₹ 5,000). One plausible explanation for this phenomenon is that lower income groups have very little to sell as in most cases what they produce suffices only for their consumption needs.

On the other hand, having a monthly income of less than ₹ 10,000 is not sufficient enough to protect them from such a practice (Mohanakumar, 2013: 176). Another important point to note here is that the incidence of distress sale was highest among the food crop cultivators as 93 percent of them testified positively to this as against just 28 percent of the cash crop farmers.

State, Political Parties and Agrarian Crisis

The respondents are highly critical of the attitude of both the state and political parties to their problems. To them, the issue is not merely that they are not offering the farming community timely help and succour, but more that they are aggrieved about their general indifference towards agriculture. The state, for instance, in its over enthusiasm to pamper other sections of the society—industrial lobby, government servants, and blue collar workers—does precious little to tackle the crisis. Further what little it does, never reaches the farmers due to the irresponsible attitude of the officials. For example, 59 percent in our sample (47 percent of cash crop cultivators and 71 percent of food crop cultivators) have complained about bureaucratic culpability and another 39.6 percent about the benefits being siphoned off by undeserving elements. In fact, this is a serious complaint raised by the food crop growers who believe that the state is more supportive of the causes of cash crop cultivators than theirs. One clear instance they point out pertains to debt relief offered by various central and state agencies.

Our data shows that among those who became the beneficiaries of debt relief, 88.71 percent belonged to cash crop cultivators and only 19 percent belonged to the other category. One important reason for this in the Kerala context is the political clout wielded by the former group due partly to their comparatively better financial position and the other part due to the existence of various Kerala Congress factions which are considered as the mouth pieces of big farmers, particularly that of the planters hailing from Kottayam district.

Fall in extension and other support services were also perceptible in the study area. There are many instances of the posts of agricultural officers lying vacant in the district as a result of which existing officers are overburdened and are unable to provide timely advice and support. Further, they themselves complain about the inadequate nature of their training (particularly in service training) because of which they fail to keep abreast of the developments taking place the field of agriculture.

So is the case with regard to scientific and technical

support from research institutions. To crown all these, the state has, of recent, started outsourcing the supply of seeds/siblings to private parties who, according to the respondents, often supply sub-quality products. Though both cash crop and food crop cultivators are worried about this, it is the latter group who are affected severely as their crops are more prone to diseases and attack by pests because of which support services of the state becomes crucial. As Reddy and Mishra (2009: 43) point out, while the emerging system of agriculture necessitates more sophisticated knowledge-based information systems, extension systems are almost defunct or in disarray.

The lapse on the part of local bodies in this matter is equally serious. It is worth noting that with the strengthening of PRIs following the 73rd and 74th Constitutional Amendments, rural local governments in Kerala are entrusted with many responsibilities—in agriculture and allied areas in particular—previously discharged by the state and its agencies. There was even a stipulation during the Peoples Plan Campaign that the allocation for goods producing sectors (here again the case of agriculture and allied areas is specifically stated) should not fall below a minimum threshold of 40-50 percent of the grants received by them [4] (Isaac and Frank: 156). This is, however, respected in its violations as the local bodies utilized such funds for improving physical infrastructure under 'popular pressure'. As a result, though agriculture got little, allocation for rural road networks improved. Harilal and Eswaran (2015:38) neatly sum up the situation thus:

In spite of [the stipulation], LGs tend to fall short of fulfilling the minimum prescribed for the goods producing sectors, especially when we consider the difference between allocation across sectors and the actual expenditure. For instance, the introduction of democratic decentralisation has resulted in an unprecedented expansion of rural/local roads networks in the state. *Kacha* roads are rarely seen now, whereas rural roads with cement concrete top are not rare to see. In our opinion, this is a reflection of the growing importance of the asset function of land. People want every piece of land to be connected by road and power lines to enhance the real estate value. It is also obvious that the virtual 'violence' of roads we see in rural Kerala does not augur well for agriculture because roads very often cut irrigation/drainage canals, convert agricultural land and facilitate conversion of land for non-agricultural purposes.

Interestingly, the respondents of our study are really appreciative of the activities of their PRIs in this regard even though it really meant financial cut for the agriculture. Their logic seems to be different—one which supports the real estate value of land. At a time when the return from land is decelerating, appreciation of sales value comes as a great relief to them, they say.

The respondents are also highly critical of political parties for their approach towards the agrarian situation. While majority [5] of them blame economic globalisation responsible for the present conjuncture, their criticism of political parties pertains to their ambivalence on the issue and the contradictory approach they adopt towards it while in power and out of it. An interesting point emerges here with regard to the attitude of the organised Left and the LDF Government on the issue. While 65.50 percent of our respondents (262 in real terms) believe that the Left as a political force is opposed to globalisation, they take a contra position with regard to the approach of the LDF Government towards it. A substantial section of the respondents (63.50 percent) do not find any significant difference between the LDF and UDF Governments in this matter. This is particularly so in the case of the younger generation, 86 percent of whom put forward such a line of reasoning.

What the respondents are trying to do is to cut a wedge between the Left in opposition and the Left in government. Such a contradiction they find in the case of other political parties as well. Thus, if one goes by their account, the political class suffers from a serious deficit of credibility in regard to both their approach towards economic globalisation in general and their attitude towards agrarian crisis in particular. To them, the sympathy of this class lies with organised interests rather than with unorganised groups like the farmers. This general distrust of the politicians and political parties has its reflection in their political behaviour also.

For instance, 41.3 percent said that they were not very much enthusiastic about voting and another 33.85 percent said that even though they were opposed to globalisation policies, that attitude would not reflect in their voting decisions as hardly any political party presented a choice in this regard or those parties who were opposed to such policies hardly had a clear cut alternative to it.

The general antipathy of the farmers towards political parties encourages them to organise independently and/or identify themselves with NGOs some of which have caste/communal undertones. Farmers' Forum is the generic name used to denote these organisations in Kerala and the most important among them are Farmers' Relief Forum, Infarm and Haritha Sena (Sharmin, 2009: 187). Additionally, there are also associations called Farmers' Clubs and, in certain areas, Neighbourhood Associations (Mohanakumar, 2013: 189). 88 percent of our respondents (93 percent of cash crop farmers and 81 percent of food crop growers) are members of one or the other of these organs and are also highly appreciative of the works done by them in such areas like mobilising farmers to fight for their causes, and against globalisation policies, promoting group farming and eliminating the intervention and exploitation of middlemen.

However, the respondents are well aware of the limitations of organisations like these in offering concrete solutions to the harmful effects of trade liberalisation. That is why even while appreciating the role played by the forums; they firmly believe that only strong state intervention could ultimately salvage the situation. They want the state to fully shoulder the responsibility of protecting agriculture by restoring a regime of subsidies, providing the much needed infrastructural facilities like irrigation, water harvesting and mechanization, and ensuring extension, research and support services. In short, they argue for declaring agriculture as a national priority rather than as a national calamity.

Notes

1. The concept of middle class in this study is identified mainly on the basis of factors like income from agriculture, size of land holding, occupational priorities and level of dependence on agriculture for livelihood.

   In terms of cropping pattern and area of land used for farming, a middle class farmer is conceived to be one who uses at least 50 per cent of his total holdings for regular agricultural purpose; in regard to ownership of land, those who possess 1 to 5 acres of cultivating land, depending on the location and the crop cultivated, belong to this class; and income-wise, this class is defined on the basis of a monthly income ranging from ₹ 3,000 to ₹ 15,000 (net income) obtained directly from agriculture. Also, dependence on agriculture and allied sectors as the sole source of livelihood is an important criteria in this regard.

   Selection of the respondents was the most difficult issue as there was no readymade list of farmers. Therefore, we depended on the beneficiary list available in various public offices viz., *Krishibhavans,* local self-government offices, Rubber Board and Spices Board. With the help of this, a sample of 400 respondents from all the five Taluks—Meenachal, Kanjirappally, Changanacherry and Vaikom—were selected on the basis of simple random sampling. Particular care was taken to choose the respondents belonging to different cropping population. Primary data was collected from these respondents by using a structured questionnaire. Personal interviews with people's representatives, political party leaders and officials connected with agriculture were also conducted to elicit their responses on specific aspects of the issue. To supplement the data collected from the field, records available in various public offices and farmers' organization were also used.
2. This is termed as 'Dutch Disease' which attributes the crisis to the resource movement and spending effect caused by migration remittances boom since the 1970s.

3. Though NABARD has fixed an annual loan target of 18 percent for agricultural sector, in most cases the target is not met because of the lackadaisical attitude of the bank officials. What the banks actually do to meet the target is to deposit money in NABARD bonds at an interest rate of 4 percent. For the banks, security of investment even at a lower rate of interest is more important than a higher rate of interest with the looming prospect of the money so disbursed being forfeited.
4. Significantly, this stipulation itself was diluted subsequently, particularly by the Twelfth Five Year Plan as a result of which the PRIs now have much leeway in deciding the amount for various sectors.
5. At the aggregate level, 240 respondents (60 percent) believe it to be harmful to the farmers' interests. While 44 (11 percent) believe it to be beneficial, the rest (116; 29 percent) are ignorant about such issues.

References

Adiseshaiah, Malcom (1994), "The Uruguay Round of Multilateral Trade Negotiations", New Delhi: Ministry of Commerce.

Andrews, Sheeba (2013), "Dynamics of Cropping Pattern Shifts in Kerala: Sources and Determinants", *Agricultural Situation in Kerala*, Vol. LXX, No. 6, September.

Baby, A.A. (1996), "Trends in Agricultural Wages in Kerala: 1960-1999", working paper, Trivandrum: Centre for Development Studies.

Balakrishnan, Pulapre (1999), "Land Reforms and the Question of Food in Kerala", *Economic and Political Weekly*, Vol. 34, No. 21, May 22-28.

Balla, G.S. and Gurmail Singh (2009), "Economic Liberalisation and Indian Agriculture: A State-wise Analysis", *Economic and Political Weekly* Vol. XLIV, No. 32, December 26-January 1.

Chakravarthy, Sukhamoy (1993), "Selected Economic Writings", New Delhi: Oxford University Press.

Deshpande, R.S. and Saroj Arora (2012), "Introduction" in R.S. Deshpande and Saroj Arora (eds.), 'Agrarian Crisis and Farmer Suicides', New Delhi: Sage Publications.

Feder, G., R.E. Just and D. Zilberman (1985), "Adoption of Agriculture Innovations in Developing Counties: A Survey", *Economic Development and Cultural Change.* Vol. 33, Issue 2,

January.

George, P.S. (2005), "Globalisation and Agricultural Transition in Kerala", Working Paper 190, Thiruvananthapuram: CDS.

Government of India (2014), "Situation Assessment Survey of Agricultural Households, NSSO 70th Round", New Delhi: Ministry of Statistics and Programme Implementation.

Government of Kerala (2013), "Twelfth Five Year Plan 2013-17", Thiruvananthapuram: State Planning Board.

—(2015), "Economic Review", Thiruvananthapuram: Planning Board.

Gulati, Ashok (2001), "Indian Agriculture and WTO: Preparing for the New Millennium", Kolkata: Indian Economic Association.

Harilal, K.N. and K.K. Eswaran (2015), "Agrarian Question and the Local Governments in Kerala", RULSG Occasional Paper, 3, Thiruvananthapuram: CDS.

Harvey, David (2007), "A Brief History of Neo-liberalism", London: Oxford University Press.

Iyer, Gopal K. (2005), "Impact of Globalisation of Farmers and Rural Poor" in S.N. Chaudhary (ed.), 'Human Rights and Poverty in India', Vol. 2, New Delhi: Concept Publishers.

Kannan, K.P. and K. Pushpangadan (1988), "Agricultural Stagnation in Kerala: An Exploratory Analysis", *Economic and Political Weekly*, Vol. 23, No. 39, September 24.

Lathika, M. (2009), "Kerala Agriculture in the Pre- and Post-Liberalization Periods", in B.N. Ghosh and Padmaja D. Namboodiri (eds.), 'The Economy of Kerala: Yesterday, Today and Tomorrow', New Delhi: Serials Publications.

Mani, K.P (2006), "Performance of Agricultural Sector in Kerala" in R.S. Sthanumoorthy (ed.), 'Kerala Economy: Achievements and Challenges', Hyderabad: ICFAI University Press.

Mohanakumar, A. (2013), "Globalisation and Changing Role of the State: A Study of Middle Class Farmers in Kottayam District", (unpublished Ph.D. Thesis), Thiruvananthapuram: Department of Political Science, University of Kerala.

Mohanakumar, S. and R.K. Sharma (2006), "Analysis of Farmer Suicide in Kerala", *Economic and Political Weekly,* Vol. 6, April 22.

Munck, Ronaldo (2005), "Globalisation and Social Exclusion: A Transformationalist Perspective", Bloomfield: Kumarian Press.

Nair, Manju S. and B. Maneesh (2015), "Dimensions of Agrarian

Crisis in Kerala", New Delhi: Synergy Books.

Oomman, M.A. (1963), "The Economics of Cropping Pattern: A Case Study of Kerala", *Indian Journal of Agricultural Economics*, Vol. 18, No. 1.

Patnaik, Prabhat (2014), "Marketing Politicians", *Frontline,* Vol. 31, No. 6, April 4

Patnaik, Utsa (2007), "The Republic of Hunger and Other Essays", Guragaon: Three Essays Collective.

Pillai, P.P. (1984), "Agricultural Development", in The Institute of Planning and Applied Research, 'Kerala Economy: Four Decades of Development', Calicut: University of Calicut.

Reddy, D. Narasimha and Srijith Mishra (2012), "Economic Reforms, Small Farmers Economy and Agrarian Crisis" in R.S. Deshpande and Saroj Arora (eds.), 'Agrarian Crisis and Farmer Suicides', New Delhi: Sage Publications.

Sharmin, Khodaij (2009), "Harvesting Despair", New Delhi: Nagari Printers.

Shyjan, D. (2007), "Public Investment and Agricultural Productivity: A State-wise Analysis of Food grains in India", Working Paper No. 387, Thiruvananthapuram: CDS.

4

Make-in-India Programme: A Perspective

Shaijumon C.S.

Introduction

"Make in India" is a major new national programme which is designed to facilitate investment, foster innovation, enhance skill development and protect intellectual property. The programme aims to build best-in-class manufacturing infrastructure in India. It encourages companies to manufacture their products in India and was launched by Prime Minister Shri Narendra Modi on September 25, 2014. *"Zero Defect Zero Effect"* is the slogan for Make in India campaign, coined by Prime Minister, which signifies production mechanisms wherein products have no defects and the process through which product is made has zero adverse environmental and ecological effects. For a country to win the tag of a developed nation, most economists argue, that it should have a turnover in its GDP (Gross domestic Production) from agro-based nation to a manufacturing nation with at least 30 percent of its GDP sourced from the manufacturing industry. Make in India campaign gives greater thrust to the massive development of manufacturing sector of the Indian economy.

Hirschman contends that deliberate unbalancing of the economy according to the strategy is the best method of development and if the economy is to be kept moving ahead, the task of development policy is to maintain tension, disproportions and disequilibrium. Investments in strategically selected industries or sectors of the economy will lead to new investment opportunities and so pave the way for further economic development. He stresses, that for development to take place, a deliberate strategy of unbalancing the economy should be adopted. This is possible by investing either in social overhead capital or indirect productive activities.

Kaldor (1966, 1967) considered manufacturing as the engine of growth; agriculture being subject to diminishing returns is not able to sustain an increasing level of production and income, and, therefore, manufacturing, without such limitations on expansion of production, is the key to sustained economic growth. The key role of manufacturing in growth is explained by Kaldor through his three famous laws, emphasizing strong causal relation between growth of manufacturing and growth of GDP, between growth of manufacturing output and growth of productivity in manufacturing and between rate of growth of manufacturing and growth of productivity in other sectors. Growth of services, according to him, was induced both by requirements of expanding industrial sector and rising levels of income.

The objective of the paper is to analyse the Make in India programme through unbalanced growth theory.

Review of Literature

Industry, particularly manufacturing, which has been observed historically to be the main contributor of growth, at least in the initial period of economic development, has played only a minor role in India's economic growth in recent years (Popola, 2005). Infrastructure investment is an important driving force to achieve rapid and sustained economic growth. The presence of sufficient infrastructure will require modernization and commercialization of agriculture and the achievement of income surpluses for capital accumulation. It can provide a basis for the expansion of local manufacturing industries, as well as enlarging markets for the outputs of these industries. The adequacy of infrastructure helps determine one country's success and another's failure in diversifying production, expanding trade, coping with population growth, reducing poverty, or improving environmental conditions

(World Development Report, 1994).

A.O. Hirschman (1958) differentiated between direct productive activities (DPA) and social overhead capital (SOC). The SOC can be seen as infrastructure and is usually defined as comprising "those basic services without which primary, secondary and tertiary productive activities cannot function". Nurkse (1958) elaborated the concept of overhead capital. According to him, "overhead investment aims at providing the services—transport, power, and water supply, which are basic for any productive activity. W.W. Rostow (1960) claimed that SOC is a pre-condition for take-off into self-sustained growth. Investment in SOC and development of those services encourages potential entrepreneurs to invest in risk-bearing business. Those SOC prepare the base for expansion of economic activities by decreasing the cost and increasing the profitability of productive activities.

Hirschman's concept of social overhead capital (infrastructure) comprises of these basic services (include all public services like transportation, communication, power, health, water supply, irrigation and drainage system) without which the primary, secondary and tertiary activities in the economy cannot function. According to Rosenstein-Rodan (1943), less developed countries are caught in a low-level equilibrium trap marked by: (i) the presence of significant economies of scale which remain unexploited due to the lack of large-scale investment, (ii) a lack of social overhead capital because private enterprises cannot internalize the positive externalities of social overhead capital, (iii) severe under-investment in other areas of large positive externalities, such as in education and on-the-job training, and (iv) disguised unemployment. Government investment is necessary to provide a "big push" to initial industrialization.

Unbalanced Growth Theory

Albert Hirschman contends that deliberate unbalancing of the economy according to the strategy is the best method of development and if the economy is to be kept moving ahead, the task of development policy is to maintain tension, disproportions and disequilibrium. Balanced growth should not be the goal, but rather the maintenance of existing imbalances, which can be seen from profit and losses. Therefore, the sequence that leads away from equilibrium is precisely an ideal pattern for development. Unequal development of various sectors often generates conditions for rapid development. More developed industries provide undeveloped industries an incentive to grow. Hence, development of underdeveloped countries should be based on this strategy.

The path of unbalanced growth is described by three phases:

Complementarity: Complementarity is a situation where increased production of one good or service builds up demand for the second good or service. When the second product is privately produced, this demand will lead to imports or higher domestic production of the second product, as it will be in the interests of the producers to do so.

Induced Investment: Complementarity allows investment in one industry or sector to encourage investment in others. This concept of induced investment is like a multiplier, because each investment triggers a series of subsequent events.

External Economies: Unbalanced growth according to Professor Hirschman generates externalities. Further explaining, we could say that the growth of industry A leads to or stimulates the growth of industry B and C and so on. Similarly, the growth of industry B and C will lead to the subsequent growth of industries E and F. Thus, the growth of strategic industries apart from providing the benefits belonging to itself also stimulates the growth of other set of industries.

Hirschman maintains that investments in strategically selected industries or sectors of the economy will lead to new investment opportunities and so pave the way for further economic development. He stresses that for development to take place, a deliberate strategy of unbalancing the economy should be adopted. This is possible by investing either in social overhead capital or direct productive activities. Social overhead capital (SOC) comprises of those basic devices without which primary, secondary and tertiary activities cannot function. This includes in it the expenditure on roads, irrigation works, power, transport and communications. The investment on these projects creates more economies and this is called divergent series of investment. Such investments are undertaken by public agencies. Direct productive activities (DPA) are those activities which are a consequence of some investment, adding to the flow of final goods and services. These series of investments are undertaken by private entrepreneurs.

Unbalancing the Economy through Make in India Campaign

Manufacturing sector is crucial for employment generation and development of India. The manufacturing sector is critical for the economy's growth as it employs 12.0 percent of the country's labour force as well as provides a transitional opportunity to the labour force in agriculture. In addition, the sector has a multiplier effect for job creation in the services sector. According to National Manufacturing Policy, 2011, every job created in the manufacturing sector creates two to three additional jobs in related activities. Industry, specially manufacturing, on the other hand, offers large scope for use of capital and technology, which could be augmented almost without limit with human effort. Kaldor (1966, 1967) considered manufacturing as the engine of growth: agriculture being subject to diminishing returns, is not able to sustain an increasing level of production and income, and, therefore, manufacturing, without such limitations on expansion of production, is a key to sustained economic growth. The most striking feature of the structural change in the Indian economy in recent decades has been the pre-eminence of the services sector as a major contributor to growth, raising its share rather sharply in the national output.

India is the world's third largest economy as per gross domestic product in PPP (purchasing power parity) terms. In terms of population, India is second in the world, with more than 1.2 billion people, out of which nearly 2/3rd of the population being in their working age. The ultimate objective of Make in India campaign is to make India a renowned manufacturing hub for key sectors. Companies across the globe would be invited to make investment and set up factories and expand their facilities in India and use India's highly talented and skilled manpower to create world class zero defect products. Main mission is to manufacture in India and sell the products worldwide.

Empowered with unique demographic advantages and guided efforts, India is poised to position itself among developed economies within the next 10-15 years. India is expected to have the largest workforce in the world by 2025. India needs an investment of about US$ 1 trillion for new infrastructure over the next few years to fulfil its reform agenda and return to the growth trajectory of about 9 percent. Growth of SOC, according to Hirschman would stimulate investment in DPA. For example, availability of cheap electricity is expected to encourage the growth of small-scale industries. Similarly, the development of irrigation works is expected to stimulate the growth of agricultural works.

Through the Make in India program, Government of India has chosen the other path of unbalancing the economy with direct productive activities or DPA. It is expected that investment in DPA would press for investment in SOC. Demand for irrigation, roads, transport and communication would increase, pressing for greater investment in these activities. It is through this process of linkages that the economy will grow. Country-level and firm-level studies generally support the view that FDI increases economic growth by bringing physical capital, advanced technology, and management expertise.

The figure on the next page demonstrates the path of

development, using the strategy of unbalanced growth. X-axis represents the investment cost in socially productive activities and Y-axis represents the investment cost in direct productive activities. AA, BB and CC represents equi-product curves indicating various combinations of SOC and DPA corresponding to the given level of national output. Higher the curve from the origin represents higher level of output. Growth process may be explained *by making initial investments either to DPA or SOC*. It is because it is assumed that in developing countries SOC or DPA cannot be expanded simultaneously.

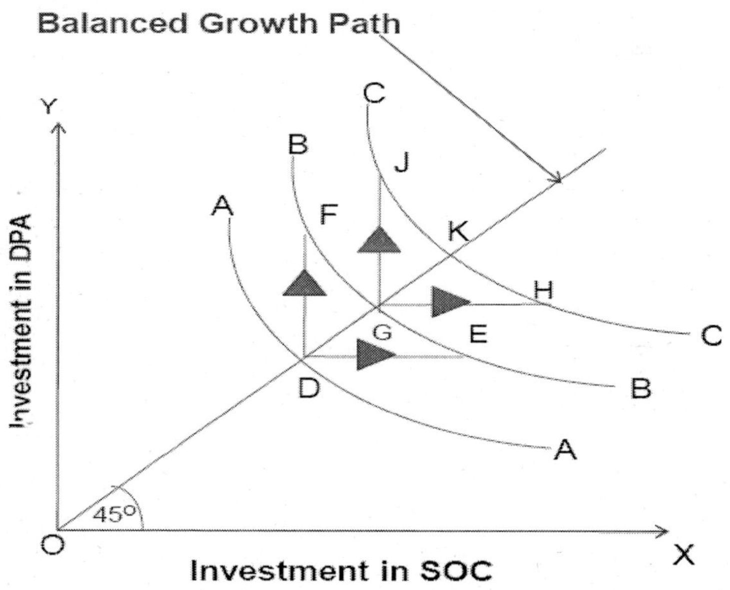

While the *former is called Development by Excess Capacity of SOC*, the *latter is known as Shortage of SOC*. Make in India campaign is instrumental to attract more investment through foreign direct investment in directly productive activities. The expansion of DPA builds up pressure on SOC. In the above figure, investment is made first in DPA and the route of development is DFGJK. We increase

DPA from D to F which results in an increase in production costs and DPA producers would realize the possibility of considerable economies through more investment in SOC facilities. Thus, SOC would increase to point E and then to equilibrium point G on BB curve implying the higher level of output. If investment is further increased from G to J, this would create pressure for more investment in SOC shifting G to H and like this the equilibrium will be struck at point K on higher iso-product curve CC, the path of growth being DGK. The success of this growth path purely depends upon how quickly and adequately SOC is responding to the DPA investment.

According to Hirschman, creating unbalances are a pre-requisite to economic growth. However, the question arises, how to identify the activities with which to create imbalances in the system. This necessitates the knowledge of inter-linkages across different sectors of the economy. Hirschman (1958) developed the concepts of backward and forward linkages for identifying the activities and analyzed their importance for economic growth. In his own words: The setting up of an industry brings with it the *availability of a new expanding market for its inputs* whether or not these inputs are supplied initially from abroad. This enhanced market exerts a backward pressure for establishing industries that supply the new entrants. He calls this process *backward linkage* effects. Every non-primary activity will induce attempts to supply through domestic production, the inputs needed in that activity. Similarly, *forward linkage effects* are created when one industry uses another industry's outputs as its inputs. Every activity that does not by its nature cater exclusively to final demands will induce attempts to utilize its outputs as inputs in some industries. Study of these linkages facilitates the choice of activities through which growth with imbalances should be generated in the system.

The sum of the backward linkage effect and the forward linkage effect gives the total linkage effect, which can be seen as the growth in new industries are induced from establishing an industry. Industries with maximum linkages ought to be developed first.

The government has identified the following twenty five industries with maximum combined linkages to give a major thrust to develop: automobiles, automobile components, aviation, biotechnology, chemicals, construction, defence manufacturing, electrical machinery, electronic systems, food processing, IT and BPM, leather, media and entertainment, mining, oil and gas, pharmaceutical, ports, railways, renewable energy, roads and highways, space, textiles and garments, thermal power, tourism and hospitality and wellness. Self-reliance is the under-current of the theory of unbalanced growth. It starts with the realistic assumption of chronic scarcity of resources in less developed countries and contemplates to initiate and accelerate the process of growth in accordance with the needs and means of the country concerned. The strategy of unbalanced growth is expected to generate greater surplus in the system. This is because of its emphasis upon the capital goods industries. This strategy is also expected to produce a very strong multiplier effect in the system, stimulating income and employment. Instead of ignoring a sector completely, this strategy focuses on unbalancing the key areas of different sectors which will help to stimulate a balanced growth in future.

Major Challenges

The government approach of unbalancing the economy through its Make in India campaign has got several challenges in its kitty. The major challenges are as under:

1. **Capital Crunch:** As a developing economy, the country is facing a huge shortage of domestic resources even for its day to day activities. Make in India policy is expecting a major share of capital through foreign investment. But the real challenge for the country is to create necessary infrastructure to facilitate the initial demands of foreign

investors.

2. **Priority Areas:** All the areas identified by the government for its Make in India campaign might not get attracted by the foreign investors. This can create a serious lapse in the growth of certain sectors and may lead to the opposite effect than that envisaged.
3. **Technology Transfer:** Proposed investment through Make in India is expected to transfer technology to the country. One of the channels of technology transfer is the trade in goods and services. The second channel is foreign direct investment (FDI). Multinational enterprises (MNEs) generally transfer technological information to their subsidiaries. Challenges like domestic absorptive capacity of technology, cultural and social factors etc. will be there in the process of technology diffusion.
4. **Trickle Down Effect:** Government of India is expecting a 'trickle down' impact through the Make in India program. Nehru-Mahalanobis strategy of economic development in India was concentrating more on 'trickle down' approach during the initial years of economic development of independent India and that strategy has failed mainly because of the poor absorptive capacity of the people and lack of their purchasing power.
5. **Lag Effect:** Creation of combined linkages through the focus on the identified sectors will have a lag effect in creating higher growth in the economy. Greatest challenge before the Government is to frame suitable policies to reduce the negative impacts of lag effect in the economy.
6. **Second Generation Reforms:** Introduction of second generation reforms through suitable changes in the markets of factors of production is a pre-requisite for attracting more foreign capital in the country. This itself is a great challenge for the country.
7. **Benefits of Demographic Advantage:** Concerted efforts are needed to convert the domestic demographic advantage into demographic dividend. This includes, investing more

in human capital like enhancement of quality of education, improvement in healthcare etc.

8. **Improvement in Social Capital**: Another great challenge is to create adequate social capital to improve the forward and backward linkages from the expected foreign investment thereby creating more employment opportunities in the domestic economy. This is also very important for absorbing new technology in the economy.

Unbalancing the economy through Make in India campaign is an approach in the right direction if it generates good quality infrastructure and attracts more foreign investment in the country. Good quality and well developed infrastructure increases the productivity potential of investments in a country and therefore stimulates FDI flows towards the country. The emphasis on manufacturing sector will generate more surplus production and creates more employment opportunities in the country. But a cautious approach is needed to identify if any dearth of investments are there in the identified sectors, which may lead to serious problems in overall development of the country. The growth centres of the world in the previous two decades like US, European Union and China are in crisis since 2008. The vacuum created by them can be filled only by a 'young' country like India. To achieve the developed country status in next three decades through Make in India campaign should be the aim of policy makers of our country.

References

Hirschman, A. (1958), "The Strategy of Economic Development", New Haven, Yale University.

Kaldor, N. (1966), "Causes of Slow Rate of Growth in the United Kingdom", Cambridge, Cambridge University Press.

——(1967), "Strategic Factors in Economic Development", Ithaca, Cornell University Press.

Nurkse, R. (1958), "International Specialization and the Concept of Balanced Growth", *Quarterly Journal of Economics*, 72(2), 183-197.

Papola, T.S. (2005), "Structural Changes in the Indian Economy: Some Implications of the Emerging Pattern", *Artha Beekshan*, Vol. 13, No. 4, March.

Rosenstein-Rodan, Paul (1943), "Problems of Industrialization of Eastern and South-eastern Europe", *Economic Journal*, 53, June-September, 202-211.

W.W. Rostow (1960), "The Stages of Economic Growth: A Non-Communist Manifesto", Cambridge.

World Bank (various years), *World Development Report*, Oxford, Oxford University Press.

Xiaolan Fu (2008), "Foreign Direct Investment, Absorptive Capacity and Regional Innovation Capabilities: Evidence from China", Global Forum of International investment, OECD.

5

Towards a Digitally-empowered Inclusive Society

Divya Balan

Introduction

Digital India is a flagship programme of the Government of India with a vision to transform India into a digitally empowered society and knowledge economy by 2020. The programme was formally launched by the Prime Minister of India on July 1, 2015 and it is scheduled to be completed by the year 2019. The core idea of this programme is to make technology central to bring about change in the society. It is envisaged as an umbrella mission of the government implemented by entire departments and coordinated by the Department of Electronics and Information Technology (DeitY) of the Ministry of Communications and Information Technology. Scope of this programme is hence all inclusive and it follows a synchronised approach. As per the Ministry of Communications and IT, Digital India is the most comprehensive programme under implementation, intended to harness the immense potential of 'Digital' to propel India forward (Siwach and Kumar, 2015). The catch phrase of the Programme is IT (Indian talent) + IT (information technology) = IT (India tomorrow). This ambitious programme can be viewed as the next stride of the already running National e-Governance Plan (NeGP) implemented to accomplish good governance in this largest working representative democracy in the world.

E-governance in India

Indian democracy being the largest and extremely diverse offers such unpredictable challenges to governance. E-governance is considered having the potential to better serve the world's second largest population by providing quality public services to its citizens, both urban and rural, rich and poor alike. According to the World Bank (2010), "e-governance or 'electronic governance' refers to the use by government agencies of information technologies such as wide area networks, the internet, and mobile computing that have the ability to transform relations with citizens, businesses, and other arms of the government. These technologies can serve a variety of different ends: convenient, effective and efficient delivery of government services to citizens, improved interactions with business and industry, citizen empowerment through access to information, or more efficient government management. The resulting benefits can be less corruption, increased transparency, greater convenience, revenue growth, and cost reductions.

Dr. A.P.J. Abdul Kalam, former President of India, (2003) had visualised e-governance in the Indian context as "*a transparent smart electronic governance with seamless access, secure and authentic flow of information crossing the interdepartmental barriers and providing a fair and unbiased service to the citizen*".

The concept of e-governance originated in India during the seventies with a focus on development of in-house government applications in the areas of defence, economic monitoring, planning and the deployment of IT to manage data intensive functions related to elections, census, tax administration etc. With this regard, the Government of India established the Department of Electronics in 1970. The subsequent establishment of the National Informatics Centre (NIC) in 1977 to electronically connect all the district headquarters was a very significant development (Raza, 2015).

The main thrust for e-governance was provided by the launching of NICNET in 1987, the national satellite based computer network. From the early nineties, with the liberalisation of economy, emphasis was given initially on automation and computerisation of departments and both

Union Government and State governments have endeavoured gradually and steadily to use information and communication technology (ICT) tools for inter-department networking, processing information and delivering services for a large number of country-wide e-governance initiatives. Maintenance of websites by government departments and other entities containing information about their objectives and vision statements, organisational structure, contact details, reports and publications was further advanced to provide online interactivity to the public by making available downloadable forms, instructions, acts, rules etc. The facility for online submission of application forms was also introduced.

As the general population also increasingly became wired, public sector institutions found greater incentives to invest in integrated service delivery and communications via digital channels. The policy emphasis was on reaching out to the rural areas of India as well as taking in greater inputs from and collaborative decisions among civil society, NGOs and private sector. A National Task Force on Information Technology and Software Development was constituted in May 1998. In 1999, the Union Ministry of Information Technology was created. In the year of 2000, IT Act was passed and e-governance got its legal reorganisation.

The NeGP was approved in May 2006 to make all government services available to citizens in their locality at affordable costs through common service delivery centres via electronic media. Its vision was to initiate SMART (Simple, Measurable, Accountable, Realistic and Time-related) projects to make SMART (Simple, Moral, Accountable, Responsive and Transparent) government (GoI, 2008). NeGP had a holistic view of integrated e-governance initiatives across the country and consisted of 27 mission mode projects (MMPs) encompassing 9 central MMPs, 11 State MMPs and 7 integrated MMPs that span multiple backend ministries and departments. It also includes 8 programme support components aimed at creating the right governance and institutional mechanisms, core infrastructure, policies and standards and the necessary legal framework for adoption of e-governance in the country (Kumar and Bhanti, 2012). The current Digital India Programme can be considered as an improved version of the NeGP and hence it would restructure and re-focus several existing schemes to match with the broader vision and mission of the Programme.

Digital India Programme: Salient Features

The Digital India Programme aims to transform our country into a digital economy with participation from citizens and businesses. Public-private-partnership (PPP) is the core preference for the execution of this initiative so as to ensure that all government services and information are available anywhere, anytime, on any device that is easy-to-use, seamless, highly-available and secured. The monitoring committee is the highest level committee of this initiative chaired by the Prime Minister under which there is a Digital India Advisory Group chaired by Minister of Communications and IT and an Apex Committee chaired by the Cabinet Secretary. For the smooth execution of this program, the Government would enhance NIC which is responsible to carry IT projects in government departments. Positions of chief information officers (CIO/CTO) in ministries and necessary senior positions within each department would be created by the DeitY for managing the initiative. Overall costs of Digital India initiative is approximately ₹ 1.13 lakh crore for ongoing schemes as well as new schemes and activities (Mishra and Others, 2015).

Vision of the Digital India Programme is centred on three key areas (DeitY, 2015). The first focal area is the creation of digital infrastructure as a utility to every citizen. This includes providing high speed internet and a unique, lifelong, online, authenticable digital identity to all citizens linked to their Aadhaar. Participation in digital and financial space would be enhanced through mobile phone and bank accounts. Easy access would be provided to the common service centres and also shareable private space on a public cloud along with safe and secure cyber space.

The second focus is the digital delivery of governance and services on demand. Seamlessly integrated across the departments, services would be available in real time from online and mobile platform. Geographical information system (GIS) would be utilised for decision support systems and development and services would be digitally transformed to single window access for improving the ease of doing business. All citizens' entitlements like documents and certificates would be made portable and available on cloud. Making financial transactions electronic and cashless is also a component of this vision.

The third vision of the Programme is the digital empowerment of citizens by extending digital literacy and universal accessibility to digital resources. Also, digital resources and services would be made available in Indian languages to improve accessibility for common people. Collaborative digital platforms for participative governance and online submission of applications and documents are yet other features of the Programme.

Nine Pillars of Digital India Programme

To fulfil these visions, the Digital India Programme comprises of nine pillars (DeitY, 2015).

The first pillar being the Broadband Highways envisaged for the penetration of high speed internet connectivity for all rural and urban areas by 2016-2017. It has mandated the communication infrastructure in new urban developments and the creation of National Information Infrastructure by integrating existing networks like National Optic Fibre Network (NOFN), National Knowledge Network (NKN) etc. to offer unified and secure cyber space to deliver services closer to home for the citizens.

Pillar two is intended to ensure Universal Access to Mobile Connectivity in the 55,669 yet uncovered villages of India.

Public Internet Access Programme entitled National Rural Internet Mission is the third pillar under which the coverage of common service centres would be extended to one in every panchayat as the viable, multi-functional end-points for service delivery and also all post offices would be converted to multi-service centres in two years' time.

Pillar four is e-governance which comprises of government process reforming that includes form simplification and removal of red tapism, for instance, by constructively utilising ICT to improve service delivery. All the databases and information as well as the public grievance redressal workflow would be made electronic.

The fifth pillar of the Digital India Programme is e-kranti or the electronic delivery of services. Under the e-education of this pillar, all schools would be connected with broadband and wi-fi. Massive online open courses and digital literacy programmes would also be initiated. Setting up of Digital Literacy Mission covering six crore rural households is envisioned to ensure transparency. E-healthcare would enable online medical consultation, medicine supply, all-India exchange of patient information and medical records which are intended to provide quality health services to all. Similarly, e-planning would implement National GIS Mission Mode Project and also GIS-based decision-making. E-farming would provide real time price information to the stake holders with the online ordering facility of resources, online cash loan and relief payment with mobile banking. E-security would offer mobile emergency services and e-finance would advance mobile banking, micro-ATM programmes etc. Likewise, e-justice would setup National Cyber Security Coordination Centre and also facilities including e-courts, e-police, e-prosecution etc.

Information for All is the sixth. This pillar largely utilises the existing infrastructure. Under this pillar, open data platform would be employed by hosting of information and documents online so that citizens can have easy access to information which is a pre-requisite for any functioning participatory democracy. Government would pro-actively engage through social media and web-based platforms like MyGov.in to inform citizens and also to ensure two-way communication between citizens and government. Online messages and e-greetings would be delivered to citizens on special occasions and programmes by the government.

The seventh pillar, Electronics Manufacturing envisions 'Target Net Zero Imports' by 2020 through policy initiatives like tax reduction, providing incentives for Start-ups, eliminating cost disadvantages etc. This pillar can be viewed as one amalgamated with the current Government's much celebrated Make in India campaign. It seeks coordinated action of many departments and fine tuning of several ongoing projects.

IT for Jobs which is the eighth pillar envisions the training of students from smaller towns and villages for IT sector jobs as well as training of service delivery agents to run viable businesses delivering IT services. Similarly, telecom service providers would be required to train rural workforce to cater to their own needs in five years. This pillar would also set up BPOs in North-Eastern states to promote the IT/ITES sector.

The final pillar is the Early Harvest Programmes which includes creation of IT platform for messages for all elected representatives and government servants, secure email within government for employees as the primary mode of communication, biometric attendance covering all central government offices in Delhi in the initial phase and providing wi-fi in all universities on NKN. All cities with population of over 1 million and tourist centres would be having public wi-fi hotspots under this scheme. All school books would be converted into e-books. SMS-based weather information and disaster alert through DeitY's mobile seva platform is yet another initiative. National Portal would be made functional for lost and found children.

If implemented properly, the Programme would surely

benefit the citizens of India, both rural and urban. Country will get boost in economic growth which will have a positive impact on employment creation, especially for the youth. It will help in deepening of Indian democracy by the use of ICT in governance. E-governance would enhance the delivery and access of government services to benefit citizens, making the system truly democratic, participative, transparent and accountable. ICT helps in improving government interactions and communication between different stakeholders in governance including G2G (Government to Government), G2C (Government to Citizens), G2B (Government to Business), G2E (Government to Employees) etc.

It also will help in better articulating citizens' needs, speedy decision-making, simplifying complicated bureaucratic procedures, better utilization of resources, cost-cutting and subsequent generation of revenue for developmental and welfare activities. The initiative also facilitates citizens' right to information and public accessibility to policy matters which is considered as the primary step towards transparency and accountability thereby combating corruption at all levels of governance (GoI, 2015). In late December 2015, the government expanded the programme and launched 22 new initiatives and broadened the scope of the existing ones. The 2016 Budget announced a number of new platforms and digital literacy training programs in rural areas and measures to spur business for Indian IT companies. However, implementing such an ambitious nationwide and all-pervading programme is not at all an easy task.

Challenges Ahead

The Digital India Programme is, by far, the biggest ever conceived initiative by an Indian Government. Due to this, impending challenges that could come in the way of successful completion of the project would be unprecedented and many. Managing the scale and complexity of the Programme itself would be a difficult task, especially since each Pillar can offer its own hurdles. Lack of a firm roadmap for implementation and availability of short span of implementation time, i.e., 5 years is a major issue. The programme is supposed to be completed by 2019 which is too early for such an ambitious, complex and multifaceted programme. Tailor made for the current Government's term, it seems just like a political agenda for the future election to win. It is an undeniable fact that basic infrastructure creation for its implementation itself would take a long time. Delays due to infrastructural deficiency could hold back its progress. Ground level implementation and sustenance are also difficult tasks if not impossible.

Since it is an umbrella project, coordination of various projects, schemes and departments is a necessity and a fail would jeopardize the whole programme. For instance, if you look at the case of the very first pillar, Broadband Highways, laying of fibre optic cables for high speed broadband connectivity under the NOFN project by the end of the year 2016 in all gram panchayats in India including those in geographically remote areas and tribal settlements is an arduous task which needs official commitment and untiring efforts. Reports say that this has been delayed several times already which led to a delay in other dependent projects and hence meeting the budget limit would be difficult. Likewise, to ensure that this NOFN is properly distributed, made functional and widely used is yet another challenge in current public service delivery scenario in India that is characterised by rampant corruption and nepotism (Ranjan, 2015; Manzar, 2015). Same is the case with the implementation of GIS. So far, deployment of GIS has been restricted to the departmental level with minimal integration (Kumar, 2015).

High cost of implementation of the Programme requires effective PPP for the timely completion of the projects. However, insufficient private participation is what we witness in India now mainly due to the long and complex regulatory processes, red tapism, corruption and hostile investment atmosphere which the government has to tackle before inviting the businesses to invest. Reports show that Indian internet start-ups are at risk as global investors and venture capitalists were apprehensive of investments. Affordability of the Government to procure network links to launch new applications and services also becomes a question at this point (Sardana, 2015).

Lack of or interrupted electric supply is a huge problem in Indian states, especially in its villages. Availability of high quality wireless internet connectivity and speed is still a mirage in many parts of the country which would slow down the creation of an internet culture necessary for the achievement of many of the pillars, especially the e-kranti. Statistics shows that India comprises of one-fourth of the world population who do not have an internet connection, especially its rural masses. Uniform and fast adoption of internet is currently lacking in India due to illiteracy, availability (cost of installations) and affordability of mobile devices and data tariffs, lack of local language content and regionally relevant apps. Already existing 'digital divide' has resulted in an unequal access to ICT and thus the information which has intensified the already existing inequalities in the society. Many a times, the whole system is controlled and the benefits of change are captured by transnational corporations and their highly skilled work force leaving behind the under-privileged and electronically disadvantaged of this country.

Many a times, projects are prioritised to benefit only certain sections of the society. Digital India can also be viewed as an elitist project which is designed as a top-down model and how far it reaches to the common people of remote rural India is a question worth asking. Participation of common people who are the real stakeholders in the decision-making processes regarding the Programme is scanty and at most times, such bodies are dominated by 'powerful' people controlling the agenda, thereby reinforcing their views but not exchanging ideas in deliberative and democratic mode.

Along with this, the fallouts of existing democratic functioning including lack of civic education, citizen apathy, the disconnection between citizens and their representatives and imperfection in societal communication are all playing their role in impeding the active public participation in democratic governance in India. Issues of lack of resource accessibility to marginalised sections of the society including women and tribal population are also worrying facts. Twinning of this project with corporate interests and investments strengthens such a doubt. Possibility of the use of ICT by the state as an agency for state propaganda and surveillance to check the critical groups and alternative voices from within and outside could be detrimental to the democratic spirit and values and could emerge as a major challenge to the hyped ideals of the Digital India Programme itself.

The recent curbs put on by the Supreme Court on the use of Aadhaar unique identification number programme has made it difficult to implement Digital India initiatives. The issue of whether Aadhaar violates privacy has been referred to a constitution bench of the Court for its decision. Government having failed so far to come up with a coherent policy on net neutrality, some critics view Digital India as a euphemism for an internet controlled by the interests of large corporations. To them, privileging a private platform over a public internet would introduce a new digital divide.

Moreover, in the Indian society, there exists a general tendency of resistance to change and the country is yet to travel a long way to shift the mindset of people, for instance, from class-based education to online education. In the case of e-governance, same kind of resistance can be seen from a section of older generation public servants due to the initial difficulty in getting used to the system and other stakeholders with vested interests (Gupta and Sharma, 2012).

Similarly, 60 percent of Indian citizens still deal in cash due to the lack of trust factor in online payments as against the e-finance envisaged by the Programme. Every day, news of cyber crimes like hacking of bank accounts or stealing of credit card information would ultimately make people reluctant in using the advantages of e-finance mechanisms (Sonia and Kumar, 2011). Cyber crime is on rise in India and hence the argument that putting the data of 1.2 billion people on the cloud could be risky and could threaten the security of individuals and the nation is of some weight.

Hence, the Digital India project demands very strong cyber network security at all levels of operation which makes the project a laborious one. Reliability, privacy protection, data confidentiality and data protection needs to be ensured. Misuse of efficiency of digital communications by targeting women, children and such other marginalised sections is also a grave concern. Environmental impact of improper electronic waste disposal is yet another grappling issue that could come in the course of the implementation of the Digital India Programme. Equally crucial is the current socio-political scenario of the country (Reddy, 2015). When the ruling government and its supporters were largely criticised for stepping into interfere with the basic rights of the people including dietary practices, academic freedom and right to dissent, the rhetoric of an empowered and inclusive society is at stake. The controversy over the appointment of a brand ambassador for the Digital India campaign is a pointer to the partisan politics and the vested interests underlying it.

Conclusion

To conclude, a well integrated—both vertically and horizontally and coordinated policy framework at both national and state level is mandatory for the implementation of this much coveted Programme. It is vital to keep up the momentum till the last stage of its execution. Sustained political support, official commitment to the visions and goals of the programme and action oriented attention is required, if it exceeds the stipulated time frame of five years, 2014-2019. Citizens should be informed, educated and engaged with about the vision, services and benefits of the Programme as many of them could be unaware of its very existence and schemes. They should be encouraged to widely use the ICT in their day-to-day affairs. Development of effective laws for cyber security is vital for trust building among stakeholders. Moreover, the whole mission should be carried out beyond mere political and party interests and focus should be primarily on the welfare of citizens. Since the programme is in its initial stage of implementation, an evaluation of its accomplishments cannot be made now. However, it is imperative to keep in mind that outcome should decide the success not the hype.

References

DeitY (2015), "Digital India", New Delhi: Ministry of Communications and IT, Government of India, available at: http://deity.gov.in/DeitY_e-book/e-gov_policy/download/Policy%20Document.pdf.

Government of India (2008), "Promoting e-Governance: The SMART Way Forward", New Delhi: Government of India, available at: http://darpg.nic.in/darpgwebsite_cms/Document/file/promoting_egov11.pdf.

Government of India (2015), "E-Governance Policy Initiatives under Digital India", New Delhi: DietY, Ministry of Communications and IT, available at: http://negd.gov.in/writereaddata/files/Digital%20Repository/Policy%20Document_0.pdf.

Gupta, Vandana and Ajay Sharma (2012), "E-Governance in India: Problems, Challenges and Prospects", *TIJ's Research Journal of Economics and Business Studies*, 1(9).

Kalam, A.P.J. Abdul (2003), Inaugural Address delivered at IIT Delhi during International Conference on E-governance, December 18, available at: https://egovindia.wordpress.com/category/president-on-egovernance.

Kumar Puneet and Prateek Bhanti (2012), "Prospects of E-Governance in India", *International Journal of Engineering and Innovative Technology*, 2(3): 335-339.

Kumar, Ridhima (2015), "Dial G for Digital India", *Governance*

Now, July 16-31, 42-46.

Manzar, Osama (2015), "Challenges and Opportunities of Digital India", Livemint e-paper Column, July 22, available at: http://www.livemint.com/Opinion/db7YgCwzQh8hJU5PVL8p3O/Digital-India-Challenges-and-opportunities.html.

Mishra, Durgesh Kumar et al. (2015), "Digital India: A Program to Transform India into a Digitally Empowered Society and Knowledge Economy", *CSI Communications*, 39(1): 7-9.

Ranjan, Akhil (2015), "'Digital India Lags Behind in World Internet Race", BBC News, September 26, available at: http://www.bbc.com/news/world-asia-india-34356300.

Raza, Ahmed (2015), "Impact of E-governance on Democratic Decentralization in India", *KILA Journal of Local Governance*, 2(1): 91-101.

Reddy, Ganapati (2015), "Beefy India's Digital Leap: Choice to Choose Android or iOS or Windows but not What to Eat!", IBN Live, October 29, available at: http://www.ibnlive.com/news/tech/beefy-indias-digital-leap-choice-to-choose-android-or-ios-or-windows-but-not-what-to-eat-1149472.html.

Sardana, M.M.K. (2015), "Vision of Digital India: Challenges Ahead for Political Establishments", ISID Discussion Notes, No. DN2015/02, 1-14, available at: http://www.isid.org.in/pdf/DN1502.pdf.

Siwach, Jyoti and Amit Kumar (2015), "Vision of Digital India: Dreams Comes True", *IOSR Journal of Economics and Finance*, 6(4): 66-71.

Sonia and Sandeep Kumar (2011), "Digital Divide in Democratic India", *IJCSET*, 1(3): 99-102.

World Bank (2010), "Asia Oceania Electronic Marketplace Association (AOEMA) Report", available at: http://go.worldbank.org/M1JHE0Z280.

6

India's Experience with International Sanction Regimes

Rishika Chauhan

Introduction

The study of economic sanctions as an instrument of foreign policy is not new. Scholars from various disciplines have attempted to explain and define the use of economic coercion in general and sanctions in particular in the domain of foreign policy. David Baldwin (1985) has provided the most authoritative survey of prior works on the use of economic coercion in the discipline of international relations. He believes that the literature on economic statecraft is scarce and there exists a "tendency to denigrate the utility of such tools" (Drezner, 1999: 10). Johan Galtung (1967), Robert Gilpin (1980) and Robert Pape (1997) have all expressed their scepticism about the success of 'such instruments'.

However, the topic has attracted the attention of various scholars from different disciplines who have evaluated economic statecraft and sanctions from different perspectives. This paper attempts to evaluate economic coercion and sanctions from the vantage point of the global south. The first section of the paper briefly defines sanctions and elucidates its history. It further narrates how sanctions were used by the League of Nations and the United Nations highlighting the gradual change in their approach—from comprehensive to targeted. Emphasising on the 'north-south' divide the recent stand of the states on unilateral coercive measures is discussed before turning to India to evaluate its approach to international sanctions.

The final section of the paper attempts to study India's perception, understanding and formulation of policy towards economic coercion in general and sanctions in particular. The main focus of the final section is to evaluate India as a sanctioner and sanctionee while tracing its history and attitude towards international sanctions.

Sanctions: An Instrument of Foreign Policy

According to David Baldwin, the "peculiar nature" of sanctions calls for a broad definition for them (Baldwin, 1998: 190). While the 'coercive' nature of this instrument of foreign policy has been highlighted by Rennack and Shuey (1998) when they define sanctions as "coercive measures imposed by one country or coalition of countries, against another country, its government or individual entities therein, to bring about a change in behaviour or policies", others have focused on the instrumental value of sanctions—"sanctions are economic instruments which are employed by one or more international actors against another, ostensibly with a view to influencing that entity's foreign and/or security policy behaviour" (Taylor, 2009: 12). For the purpose of this study, sanctions are defined as coercive economic, diplomatic or military instruments imposed by one state or an international organisation to change the behaviour or policies of another state or entity. Economic sanctions are imposed in the form of trade embargoes, asset freeze, import restrictions etc.; diplomatic sanctions include limitations or cancellation of high-level government visits or expulsion or withdrawal of diplomatic missions. Military sanctions target the military sector of a country, and may include arms embargo or total cut off of military supplies.

Megarian Decree imposed by the Athenian Empire on Megara in 432 B.C., is the oldest documented example of peacetime economic sanction. The decree, primarily a response to Megara's cultivation of sacred land—was directed against the citizens of Megara, barring them from trading in the Athenian Empire. Since then many states over the centuries have used sanctions to arm-twist and change the behaviour of target states. International organisations, throughout the 20th and 21st centuries, used sanctions to impose their positions. The League of Nations first imposed sanctions in 1921 against Yugoslavia when the latter invaded Albania. The organisation imposed or threatened to impose economic sanctions only four times during its existence (Hufbauer et al., 2007: 20). Under Chapter VII of the United Nations Charter, the United Nations (UN) can also impose sanctions in the event of any "threat to peace, breach of peace or an act of aggression". The 1990s was called the 'Sanction's Decade' in the UN as the number of sanction cases increased from two in the Cold War period to 50 between 1990 and 2000.

UN sanctions evolved after the end of Cold War, acquiring a more focused outlook, targeting individuals, groups or entities to mitigate collateral damage (Cortright and Lopez, 2002: 6). Post-Cold War, the nature of issues that sparked sanctions also changed significantly. As UN cases involving conflicts within the states increased from 25 percent to 53 percent post-Cold War, sanctions also started to be used to strengthen the UN's efforts to contain intra-state conflicts. The cases that did not aim at stopping conflicts, usually dealt with states with terrorist links or regimes pursuing weapons of mass destruction—particularly Iraq, Libya, Iran and North Korea (Elliott, 2009: 90). Currently, the UN has 10 sanctions regimes in place in the following states: Eritrea and Somalia; Iraq; Liberia; the Democratic Republic of the Congo; Cote d'Ivoire; Sudan; Syria; the Democratic People's Republic of Korea; Iran; and against Al-Qaeda members (UN, 2013).

States and Sanctions: North-South Divide

Among states, the US has imposed the highest number of unilateral sanctions in the world. Over the years, sanctions have emerged as a favoured policy tool of the US and served a number of purposes, ranging from signalling disapproval, pleasing domestic constituencies, to meaning actual harm

(Haass, 1997). The US has a well-laid and articulate policy on international sanctions. Primary sanctions that directly aim the target and secondary sanctions which are enforced on the bodies that do not conform to established sanction regimes, are both enacted through US domestic laws or presidential executive orders. The idea of economic sanctions as an instrument of policy was introduced by President Woodrow Wilson in 1919. While making a case for the League of Nations, Wilson discussed sanctions, arguing, "apply this economic, peaceful, silent, deadly remedy and there will be no need for force" (Hufbauer et al., 2007: 1).

Through the 20th and 21st centuries, the US imposed a number of economic sanctions. According to Peterson's Institute of International Economics, the US imposed economic sanctions more than 101 times in the 20th century. Acknowledging this fact, then President Bill Clinton in 1998 asserted that the US had become "sanctions happy" (Hufbauer, 1998). Later, George W. Bush and Barack Obama would carry on with this legacy and place a number of sanctions on various entities. Currently, the US has a number of sanctions regimes in place: Cuba, Iran, North Korea, Cote d'Ivoire, Syria, Sudan and a number of other states, drug traffickers and terrorist organisations are under US sanctions.

Sanctions today have not only gained acceptability but also popularity among many Western states. However, China, Russia and various developing states have raised their objections to sanctions, especially unilateral ones. On March 15, 2012, India, along with Russia, China and 32 other states, voted in favour of a UN Human Rights Council resolution (A/HRC/19/L.12) that lucidly discussed human rights and unilateral coercive measures. According to the resolution: "Unilateral coercive measures in the form of economic sanctions can have far-reaching implications for the human rights of the general population of targeted States, disproportionately affecting the poor and the most vulnerable classes. Long-term unilateral coercive measures may result in social problems and raise humanitarian concerns in the States targeted" (UN General Assembly, 2013).

Most of the European Union member states and the US voted against the resolution. The developing states have often argued that sanctions infringe upon sovereignty. Though developing states cannot be taken as a monolithic entity while exploring their perspectives on sanctions, in general, academics in many developing states seem sceptical of the true intentions of the sanctioner (Chenoy, 2013).

The UN General Assembly has taken a keen interest on the issue of sanctions. At the 2005 World Summit, the UN General Assembly called upon the Security Council thus: "To ensure that fair and clear procedures exist for placing individuals and entities on sanctions lists and for removing them, as well as for granting humanitarian exemptions" (UN World Summit, 2005).

However, specialists have pointed out that what constitutes "fair and clear procedures" is contested, and its determination depends on both legal and political arguments. The final judgement always rests with the Security Council (Biersteker and Eckert, 2006).

Unlike the US, China, is known as an opposer of economic sanctions, especially unilateral ones (Reilly, 2012: 121). It has often termed sanctions as 'immoral' and 'illegal'. The country is known for criticising unilateral sanctions and occasionally vetoing them at the United Nations. However, China is beginning to change its policy and employing its economic might to attain foreign policy objectives (Reilly, 2012: 122). Unlike US, the Chinese policy on sanctions is not formalized through domestic laws or presidential orders. Their policy on the issue is vague, which often provides flexibility to the leadership to impose and repeal sanctions without much justifications and international limelight.

Like China, India has not been vocal about its policy towards international sanctions. It has been argued that, traditionally, India has viewed sanctions as a diplomatic tool that "does not serve any purpose" (Chaudhury, 2010).

However, India's support for various multilateral sanctions regimes is evident, especially the ones against terrorist groups (Puri, 2011). Though, with the opening up of the Indian economy, the state has become a pertinent player in the arena of economic statecraft and India's views are given sufficient consideration at the international level, but unlike the permanent members of the UNSC, its stand on sanctions cases does not carry much weight in the UN. Yet, studying Indian foreign policy and discourse closely reveals that the subject of international sanctions has been amply discussed and debated by Indian leaders, policymakers and economists.

India and Sanctions

Indian foreign policy has evolved with time. It is often divided into three distinct historical sections, to bring out the underlying values of each phase. The first section is called the 'idealist' phase (1947-1962), the second is characterized by a 'self-help' approach (1962-1991) and the third is believed to be more 'pragmatic' (1991 onwards) than the rest (Ganguly and Pardesi, 2009). The 21st century, has witnessed considerable changes in Indian foreign policy.

A 'new' policy seems to be emerging which holds its core values dear but realises that India's role in the world has dramatically transformed. The situation calls for a policy that is more adaptable to internal and external environment compared to its former avatars (Mohan, 2009). As we examine the future challenges confronting India, it is important to take a step back and study the instances when India imposed sanctions on other states and entities, when sanctions were imposed on it and how it reacted to sanctions when they were placed against other states.

India has not shied away from using economic tools to further its foreign policy goals (Khurshid, 2013). Nonetheless, it is one of the few states in the world with a unique position, having played the roles of both sanctioner and sanctionee. As the Indian economy grows and becomes more connected with the world economy, it finds itself potent enough to use economic coercion and connected enough to face the same. An emerging power, India's international interests are growing; simultaneously, it has had difficulties dealing with the growing frequency and intensity of international sanctions. Of late, the issue of Iranian sanctions has come to light, and consequently India has had to manage the tension between the international approach to the issue and its own foreign policy interests. Hence, the question of international sanctions has begun to acquire some salience in the conduct of India's foreign policy.

Sanctions in India's Foreign Policy

India's foreign policymakers have been prudent enough to recognise the importance of economic coercion as an instrument of foreign policy. Economic sanctions were discussed as early as in 1936, when the foreign policy discourse was beginning to take shape. Highlighting the broad outline of Indian National Congress's foreign policy, Ram Manohar Lohia, the first secretary of the party's foreign affairs department, announced that India would not hesitate to use economic sanctions against an aggressor, to support "national, democratic and socialist forces" around the world (Prasad, 1960: 134). Soon after, in May 1938, the architect of Indian foreign policy, Jawaharlal Nehru, discussed sanctions elaborately while elucidating the Congress's attitude towards collective security.

Emphasising Indian foreign policy's leaning towards peaceful methods to solve international problems, he declared: "In a world full of war and preparations for war, India stands significantly as a country which has deliberately based its policy on peace and non-violence. How far it is possible to apply these methods in the international sphere today is difficult to say. But it must be remembered that the non-violence of the Indian struggle is not a weak, passive and ineffective pacifism. It is a dynamic thing with sanctions behind it and if the world is to progress in culture and civilization, it will have to adopt peaceful methods of solving its problems" (Nehru, 1938: 4).

Nehru believed that for any system of collective security to be successful it had to be backed by sanctions. Stressing that the failure to invoke sanctions would mean allowing complete freedom to the aggressor, he said: "To have no sanctions is to allow free play to the aggressor, and ultimately to bow to his will. That cannot be agreed to for that means no collective security. It means the law of the jungle".

Moreover, Nehru explained that among various types of sanctions, the economic ones were most effective and had the advantage of being both powerful and peaceful, at the same time. Though he acknowledged that the effect of sanctions might not be immediate, he had full faith in its "far-reaching" nature and its ability to change the behaviour of the aggressor. Nehru did not rule out the use of military sanctions (Nehru, 1938: 4).

Later, A. Appadorai, a renowned political scientist of that time, examined three fundamental ideas of India's foreign policy. He listed "whole-hearted co-operation with the United Nations and unreserved adherence in both spirit and letter, to the Charter governing it" as the primary element of India's foreign policy (Appadorai, 1949: 40). He also believed that India had cooperated sincerely with the system of collective security enshrined in the UN charter, implying its adherence to sanctions.

Even before India's Independence, economic coercion in the form of sanctions was used by the Indian National Congress and the British government to pursue their foreign policy objectives. In 1939, the Indian National Congress, the party which formed the government post-Independence, initiated a boycott of Japanese goods throughout India as a protest against Japan's invasion of China. It was a gesture extended by the leaders of the party in order to show sympathy to China. Assistance was sent to China in the form of men, money, materials, and medical missions. This decision of the Indian National Congress was also an attempt to show that the party had its own foreign policy (Dixit, 1992: 539). Although it was executed more with the purpose of signalling displeasure over Japan's actions than actually meaning economic harm on the target, the episode had significant implications for future policies. After all, this happened at a time when India's international consciousness was growing, though its worldview was still in its infancy.

Another sanctions case that can be said to have been initiated before India's Independence was the economic boycott of Israel. Being a sympathiser of the Palestinian cause and dependent on the Arabs, India supported the Arab trade and oil boycott of Israel (Feiler, 2012). As a consequence, India limited its economic transactions with Israel right up to January 1992, when it established full and normal diplomatic relations with the State. To examine how this tradition influenced India's policies post-Independence, it is important to delve further and analyse India's policies and positions towards sanctions after 1947.

India as Sanctioner

Seven years after the Japanese trade boycott, another instance of sanctions came to light. On this occasion, however, political will and might were both channelised to undertake a formal decision which was driven by a strong cause. In 1946, though still under the jurisdiction of the British crown, the Government of India imposed economic and political sanctions on South Africa by initiating the termination of trade agreement and withdrawing its high commissioner from the independent Commonwealth member. According to a statement released by the Indian High Commission in South Africa, the sanctions were enforced to protest against the discrimination of the Indian community living in South Africa. The Viceroy's executive council member, Dr. Narayan Bhaskar Khare, played an instrumental role in bringing about the sanctions (Llyod, 1991). The sanctions were launched to object to the Segregatory Areas Reservation and Immigration and Registration Bill of 1925, which was further "pegged" by the Trading and Occupation of Land Restriction Act of April 1943 (Llyod, 1991: 709). These sanctions did not only have a symbolic purpose of disapproving of South African policies towards Indians but were also meant to have an economic impact on the country, which in turn came at an economic cost for India.

On May 1, 1948, there followed a sanctions episode of a different nature. After India's Independence, the Nizam of Hyderabad expressed his intention to stay independent. To coerce the largest princely state to join the Indian Union, the Government of India imposed a series of financial and trade sanctions on Hyderabad beginning in July 1948 (Guruswami, 2008). Through a cablegram dated August 20, 1948, the Nizam of Hyderabad took the issue to the UN Security Council. Addressing the President of the UNSC, the cablegram stated:

"The Government of Hyderabad, in reliance on Article 35, paragraph 2, of the Charter of the United Nations, requests you to bring to the attention of the Security Council the grave dispute which has arisen between Hyderabad and India, and which, unless settled in accordance with international law and justice, is likely to endanger the maintenance of international peace and security. Hyderabad has been exposed in recent months to violent intimidation, to threats of invasion, and to crippling economic blockade which has inflicted cruel hardship upon the people of Hyderabad and which is intended to coerce it into a renunciation of its independence"(U.N. Doc S/986).

However, the imposition of sanctions was short-lived and on September 16, 1948, the Indian Army moved in and occupied Hyderabad. In November, 1949, the Nizam signed the Instrument of Accession to the Indian Union. The efficacy of sanctions is highly debated in this case. Robert A. Pape considers it a case of "military conquest" and not of economic coercion (Pape, 1997: 111). Nevertheless, this was the first time when sanctions were used by the Indian state for the purpose of political unification. It was the peaceful nature of this tool of foreign policy that made the Indian state choose sanctions before turning to other options.

It was also in 1949 when India imposed a trade embargo on Pakistan as it refused to devalue its currency with respect to the US dollar. In 1948-49, before the imposition of sanctions, about 70 percent of Pakistan's trading transactions were with India, and 63 percent of India's exports went to Pakistan. Economists believe that these sanctions made Pakistan seek new and distant markets in Japan and the US. It is also said to be a "transformational experience" for Pakistan, as after facing the sanctions, it intensely tried to acquire an industrial base (Burki, 2011: 1).

The Government of India again used sanctions in 1954, this time for the purpose of assimilating a province into Indian territory: the target was Goa, a colony of the Portuguese since 1505. In 1954, when tensions and protests started growing in Goa, the Government of India imposed a trade embargo against the territories of Portuguese Goa and closed its consulate in Panjim, which had been operating since 1947. The government's decision was in accordance with its policy of following peaceful methods for political integration. On July 26, 1955, speaking in the Lok Sabha, Prime Minister Jawaharlal Nehru said: "There is no one in this House who requires any argument in justification of India's claim to Goa. It is obvious. There is hardly any question that has come before this House which had such unanimous approval or agreement. The only questions that have arisen are as to the steps that might be taken to give effect to India's claim. Even there, so far as I can understand, it is by and large the opinion of this House that the methods should be peaceful" (Nehru, 1955: 111).

Nevertheless, it was again the military, which occupied Goa in 1961 and helped in its incorporation into the Indian territory. India used sanctions as a signal of disapproval on November 12, 1965, as it imposed diplomatic sanctions in the form of non-recognition against the government of Rhodesia. In this case, India was following suit and supporting the UN's condemnation of the "illegal racist minority regime" of Rhodesia. Germany, Norway, Sweden, Denmark, Israel, Japan and Turkey also imposed similar sanctions on Rhodesia (UNSC Resolution 216).

In 1987, India again took a firm stand and reached out for the protection of the rights of the people of Indian descent, this time in Fiji. On September 25, 1987, a coup d'état installed Lieutenant Colonel Sitiveni Rabuka, as the head of the country. One of the reasons behind the coup was to keep the Indo-Fijians from gaining political power. The annulment of the Constitution was a subsequent step to marginalise the Indo-Fijian population of Fiji (Fogleman, 2008). Understanding the situation, India immediately imposed trade sanctions on Fiji and also checked its diplomatic ties with the state. Like in the South African case, India lobbied in the UN and the Commonwealth of Nations for sanctions against Fiji. The sanctions continued till 2001 as there was another coup in 2000. However, in 2006 when a third coup took place, India did not impose sanctions on Fiji. This time, Ajay Singh, the Indian High Commissioner in Fiji, claimed that India believed in "engagement rather than isolation" (Singh, 2007).

In 1989, India imposed unilateral trade sanctions on Nepal to check its growing tilt towards China. Responding to Nepal's purchase of anti-aircraft guns from China, India partially closed its borders to Nepal for thirteen months. This was a peculiar case, as the subject of security was linked to economic and transit issues. The overall stand taken by India was that if Nepal sought a special economic relationship and privileges from India it had to accept a special security relationship as well (Garver, 1991: 958). The spokesperson of the External Affairs Ministry then stated: "India has always valued the special relationship with Nepal as embodied in the 1950 Treaty of Peace and Friendship...For the last four decades, India has done everything possible to live up to the letter and spirit of the treaty. Good neighbourliness implies a degree of mutual sensitivity and concern for the interests of both countries. This is particularly necessary if the special relationship between India and Nepal is to be maintained" (India News No. 7/89).

According to United States General Accounting Office Report, titled "Economic Sanctions: Effectiveness as Tools of Foreign Policy", the sanctions succeeded in changing Nepal's behaviour to a great extent, leading to the suspension of its arms purchase from China. As a consequence of the sanctions, discontentment among the people grew, and over time the public became disillusioned with their existing king. In 1990, the Nepali Congress called for strikes which eventually resulted in the collapse of the monarchy.

Thirteen months after India sanctioned Nepal, King Birendra gave up power in favour of a pro-democratic government. Sanctions were lifted on July 1, 1990 (Crossette, 1990). The new government agreed to consult India while deciding on defence issues. It is believed that the monarchy in Nepal collapsed under the impact of Indian sanctions. This case is regarded as one of the examples of efficient economic statecraft (Mukherjee, 2004).

Responding primarily to Pakistan's inaction against two militant groups, Jaish-e-Mohammed and Lashkar-e-Taiba, blamed for a suicide attack on the Indian Parliament, India imposed sanctions on Pakistan. According to a report published by the Public Diplomacy Division of the Ministry of External Affairs, the Indian High Commissioner was withdrawn from Islamabad, the strength of its mission was reduced, and overhead flights were banned.

The Lahore-New Delhi bus and train services were also suspended. Announcing the sanctions in a statement issued on December 27, 2001, Jaswant Singh, the then External Affairs Minister, explained: "Regrettably India's serious concerns about all the ramifications of the December 13 attack on our Parliament have not been fully grasped in Pakistan. The depth of concern in India, the totality of rejection by the entire cross-section of our country's opinion of Pakistan's continued sponsorship of cross-border terrorism, and its promotion of terrorism as an instrument of state policy has also not been sufficiently appreciated.

That is why it is doubly regrettable that attempts to dupe the international community with cosmetic half measures, non-measures, or even fictitious incidents are still being made. This is not acceptable. Terrorism can simply not be justified on any grounds, or under any name. It must be eradicated fully. The Government of India therefore has no option but to take the following further steps".

As soon as India announced the sanctions, Pakistan counter-scored with its reciprocal measures (Space Daily, 2001). Thereafter, Pakistan banned the two groups in January 2002 (BBC, 2013). This decision was welcomed in India, and on January 13, 2002, the External Affairs Minister announced: "We welcome the now declared commitment of the Government of Pakistan not to support or permit any more the use of its territory for terrorism anywhere in the world, including in the Indian State of Jammu and Kashmir. This commitment must extend to the use of all territories under Pakistan's control today".

India as the Target of Sanctions

Besides, donning the role of a sanctioner, India has also been subjected to international sanctions. India has been sanctioned or threatened by sanctions more than once (Weiss, 2007: 430). India became the target of international sanctions in 1965, when US announced an arms embargo on India and Pakistan during the war between the two. The sanctions were partially lifted in 1966 and fully in 1967 (Cohen, 1976: 56).

In response to India's 1974 (Pokhran I) nuclear test, nuclear equipment and material embargo was imposed on India. Immediately, after the test, Canada announced the suspension of nuclear cooperation with India, though nuclear ties between the two were totally severed only in 1976 when India refused to

accept safeguards on all nuclear activities (Spectre, 1985: 61).

Great Britain and Japan also, almost immediately cut bilateral aid to India. From 1975 to 1977, US voted against loans to India at International Development Association, though it was overruled every time. Under the provisions of 1978 Nuclear Non-Proliferation Act, US announced the prohibition of nuclear aid to India after March 1980.

However, in 1980, President Jimmy Carter used his right to waive sanctions and permitted a fuel shipment for two reactors at Tarapur. After US intelligence reports suggested that India might be preparing for another nuclear test, the second shipment was withheld. During this time, New Delhi claimed that Washington could not stop fuel supply as it was bound by 1963 Indo-American Nuclear Trade Agreement. Nevertheless, the Reagan administration terminated the US supply relationship in 1982, and France took its place (Spector, 1985: 60).

In the 1990s, US adopted an aggressive policy towards India, with the intention to, "cap, roll back and eventually eliminate", Indian nuclear and missile capabilities (Holum, 1994). As a consequence, India came under tremendous pressure to modify its nuclear and missile posture. During this time, US opposed the deployment of the short-range Prithvi missile and development of the medium-range Agni missile. To check India's growing capabilities, US imposed sanctions on India's civilian space program in 1992, bearing in mind the potential for cryogenic rocket technology to contribute to India's ballistic missile capability (Choudhury, 2008: 8). The same year, Nuclear Supplier's Group (NSG) barred India from engaging in nuclear commerce with the world (Varadarajan, 2008). This was the result of the group strengthening its guidelines, by the addition of a list of dual-use technologies and more stringent measures.

The most widely known and discussed sanctions against India were placed by the US, after its second nuclear tests (Pokhran II) in May 1998. The sanctions, imposed under Section 102(b) of the Arms Export Control Act (AECA) included prohibitions on foreign assistance, weapons sales and licences, foreign military financing, government credit, guarantees and export of certain controlled goods and technology. Humanitarian aid, food and agriculture exports, food assistance, private bank loans for purchase of food and agricultural commodities and certain transactions involving intelligence activities were excluded from the list (Grimmett, 2001). Some non-statutory sanctions, restricting high level visits and military to military contacts were also imposed in accordance with President Clinton's administration policy (Spector, 2012).

In July 1998, the Congress amended portions of these sanctions and allowed the President the authority to waive particular sanctions. Using this authority, President Clinton waived statutory restrictions, in the context of US government programs and commercial transactions involving the two countries on October 27, 1999. On September 22, 2001, after the September 11 attacks on the World Trade Centre, President Bush waived sanctions imposed under Section 102(b) of AECA, and the Export-Import Bank Act (Grimmett, 2001).

The same year, Pakistan retaliated to India's 2001 sanctions imposed on it citing Pakistan's inaction in punishing the terrorist groups accused of attacking the Indian Parliament. Pakistan reciprocated by placing sanctions on India, similar to the kind imposed on it.

India's Response to Sanctions

To get a clear idea about India's attitude towards international sanctions, it is important to look into India's responses to sanctions imposed on other states. With the end of Cold War, US assumed an important role in the UN. On August 6, 1990, UNSC placed an oil embargo and comprehensive trade sanctions on Iraq, marking the beginning of the 'Sanctions Decade'.

India, at the threshold of economic reforms, opposed these sanctions bearing in mind the traditionally friendly relations and commercial ties with Iraq. However, as the decade progressed, India supported many UNSC resolutions. It seldom opposed the resolutions, though sometimes abstained from voting.

Supporting the sanctions placed on states/entities with which India shares good relations or commercial interests have not been easy for India. Over the years, India has been dabbling with interests and obligations especially with respect to sanctions imposed on its neighbours. Unlike US, India does not have an overt foreign policy and supporting domestic laws that emphasise on goals like democracy promotion and non-proliferation.

However, India has stood by and endorsed international laws and norms in its capacity. While analysing India's response to sanctions, it is important to throw light on episodes wherein India had interests and good relations with the target states. In this context, India's stand on the unilateral sanctions imposed on three of its neighbours, Burma, Sri Lanka and Iran is important.

Burma has been a target of broad Western sanctions primarily from 1988, yet the most stringent sanctions on Burma have been enforced by the US. Accusing Burma of "committing large scale repression of democratic opposition", US imposed sanctions on May 20, 1997 under Executive Order 13047.

According to a report published by the US State Department of the Treasury Office of Foreign Assets Control, these sanctions prohibited US companies from making new investments or assisting Burma in attracting investments. On July 28, 2003, the President signed the Burmese Freedom and Democracy Act into law, which aimed at restricting financial resources of ruling military junta. In 2007 and 2008, more executive orders were passed.

In addition to the orders, the President signed the Tom Lantos Block Burmese JADE (Junta's Anti-Democratic Efforts) Act into law in 2008, which further tightened the sanctions. European Union, UK, Australia and Canada also imposed sanctions on Burma for the same reason. Yet, the issue failed to be a cause of much concern in Burma's neighbourhood. In fact, China rushed in to fill the void that the Western sanctions had created. Though India maintained that it stood for democracy in Burma, it did not base its relations on a demand for democracy.

In 2006, Pranab Mukherjee, the then External Affairs Minister, stated that India could not "export democracy" in its neighbourhood and it had to deal with the governments as it existed (Routray, 2011: 318). Interestingly, the top Indian officials understood Burma's situation quite differently, compared to their Western counterparts.

In an article, Shyam Saran, former Foreign Secretary and Ambassador to Myanmar explained that the, "enduring hostility", that the regime had faced from the US and its Western allies, had resulted in a sense of "siege and paranoia" among the generals. In the eyes of military junta, Suu Kyi had become "an instrument in the hands of West to force a regime chang".

It will not be wrong to say that the Indian government has preferred to maintain distance from the US-led sanctions and censure against the military junta, and maintained silence along with China and ASEAN countries (Saran, 2010).

In contrast to the Burmese case, India's position on Sri Lanka has been different. Various Indian political parties have taken a firm stand on the Sri Lankan government's alleged abuse of power during the 26-year civil war. India also backed a US-sponsored resolution of March 22, 2012 at the UN Human Rights Council calling on Sri Lanka to again probe claims against Sri Lankan army, and Tamil Tiger guerrillas for committing war crimes during the conflict that ended in 2009 (Macaskill and Freedman, 2012). Recently, the issue again surfaced with US circulating a proposed resolution against Sri Lanka at the UN Human Rights Commission in March 2013. Early this year, a number of demands were being made in

India regarding the Sri Lankan issue.

Some groups in India were advocating economic sanctions against Sri Lanka and asking the Indian government to support any such sanction regime imposed by other bodies or states. In February 2013, the Tamil Nadu governor, K. Rosaiah urged the Indian government not only to place economic sanctions but also collaborate with other states to design a sanction regime against the Sri Lankan government to address the issue of maltreatment and discrimination and displacement of Tamils in Sri Lanka (Times of India, 2013).

AIADMK supremo J. Jayalalithaa and DMK president M. Karunanidhi, both made similar demands (Times of India, 2013). Though the Indian government had not taken a stand, pro-sanctions public opinion was very evident in this case.

Presently, Iran is under multiple unilateral and multilateral sanctions which primarily aim at checking Iran's nuclear program. Iran has been largely accused of violating international law, non-proliferation treaty obligations, refusing to allow International Atomic Energy Agency (IAEA) to inspect its uranium enrichment facilities and rejecting diplomatic solution, consequently creating nuclear proliferation risks (UNSC Resolution 1696, 2006).

UN imposed sanctions on Iran in 2006 under Article 41 of Chapter VII of the Charter, forbidding the supply of nuclear-related materials and technology (UNSC Resolution 1737). Existing sanctions were further tightened and expanded in 2007 and 2008, through Resolution 1747, 1803 and 1835, targeting chiefly Iran's weapons of mass destruction (WMD) program.

After failed negations in 2009, UNSC passed Resolution 1929 on June 9, 2010, that adopted more stringent steps to check Iran's activities. Resolution 1984, passed on June 9, 2011, extended the mandate of the Iran Sanctions Committee's Panel of Experts for one year and Resolution 2049, passed on June 7, 2012, renewed the same mandate for thirteen months. Though initially apprehensive, India has implemented UN sanctions (Katzman, 2013).

As India's nuclear isolation ended and it assumed a more 'responsible' role in world affairs, it became obvious that its decisions with respect to Iran would involve more considerations than before. One of the consequences of the "transformation" was New Delhi's reorganisation of the need to defend the existing international order, even if it was "unjust from India's own past criteria" (Mohan, 2010: 141).

Amid news of Iranian uranium enrichment, India came out with a clear stand on the issue, consistent with its new obligations. In 2010, while addressing the members of Indian and Iranian think tanks, the Indian Foreign Secretary Nirupama Rao claimed, India did not wish to see the spread of nuclear weapons in West Asia but at the same time believed that Iran had a right to use nuclear energy for peaceful purposes, while fulfilling its international obligation as a non-nuclear weapon state under the NPT (Rao, 2010).

India opposed unilateral sanctions on Iran citing their "extra-territorial nature" but reassured its West Asian friends and the US that its interest in Iran would not be in contradiction with the relationship India shares with them. It has maintained that International Atomic Energy Agency (IAEA) provides the best framework to resolve the issue (Dikshit, 2010).

However, a significant characteristic of US-led sanctions regime against Iran is its stress on secondary sanctions, which involve supplementary economic restrictions intended to restrain non-US citizens and companies abroad from undertaking business with a target of primary US sanctions. Aimed at completely isolating the target, secondary sanctions have certainly diversified the scope of the sanction regime. Secondary sanctions have made investors not only think twice before engaging with Iran, but also deterred them from investing and engaging with Iran. The Indian state, individuals and companies have also been affected by US secondary sanctions against Iran and the government has reportedly diminished oil purchase from Iran as a consequence of the sanctions (The Financial Express, 2013).

Conclusion

Sanctions always come at a cost, not only for the target but also the entity that imposes them. At the end of the day, sanctions are a political tool, entailing costs that are not only economic in nature. Today, sanctions are understood in different ways especially in the discipline of international relations.

According to Robert Gilpin, a renowned international political economy scholar, sanctions constitute a rigorous manipulation of economic relations to achieve political aims (Merom, 2001). Meanwhile, David Baldwin, an eminent political scientist, believes that sanctions are merely a part of a larger set of policy instruments available to foreign policy makers (Baldwin, 1998).

Sceptics argue that sanctions or threats of sanctions can send messages of fear, anxiety, and resentment, rather than of a serious attempt at solving the issue at hand. The efficacy and impact of sanctions is also highly debated across various academic disciplines. Nevertheless, the general view about sanctions is that their use is likely to increase in the future. However, it is important to understand the implications of sanctions before putting them to use. Sanctions have become a means for US to pursue its 'chicken soup diplomacy', and many other Western countries are seen toeing the line.

While emphasis is being laid on making the sanctions bite, it is forgotten that the ultimate aim of sanctions is to change the policy of the target. To achieve that end, it is not merely an impact that can coerce the target, but a host of other factors that depend on the nature and type of the target.

While examining the views of the global south on sanctions, its concern about the comprehensive and extra-terrestrial nature of sanctions are visible. The global south has raised its objections to this instrument of coercion, yet has not been able to affect the policies of the developed West. Forming a bloc and opposing unilateral coercive measures in general and sanctions in particular indeed seems like an attractive idea, yet considering that each state in the south has its individual interests and dealings with the developed states, such a plan will be hard to execute especially in the coming years when interconnectivity among states is predicted to increase.

In the context of sanctions, India's considerations for interests and responsibilities both are visible. Over the years, India has emerged as an important player in the arena of global politics. Domestically, foreign policy is an important issue for India's electorate and the Indian government has spent substantial time and effort in developing its policy and relations with the rest of the world.

With the development of its economy and expansion of its relations, India is more interconnected and relevant than ever before. Its acceptance in the global nuclear order has also made it attentive to new responsibilities and obligations. It cannot be denied that India's stand on unilateral sanctions has often aligned more with the southern part of the world than the West.

India has been sceptical of the use of unilateral sanctions, but recent events have called for adaptation rather than an outright rejection of unilateral sanctions. It cannot be overlooked that this instrument of statecraft has been employed by India in the past and is still available to the state. With growing external and internal pressures, it remains to be seen what kind of policy India adopts with respect to economic coercion in general, and sanctions in particular: assertive and vocal in the lines of the US or silent yet strong like its neighbour China.

References

Appadorai, A. (1949), "India's Foreign Policy", *International Affairs*, 25(1): 37-46.

Baldwin, David and Robert Pape (1998), "Evaluating Economic

Sanctions", *International Security*, 23:2, 189-198. BBC India Profile: Chronology, available at: http://www.bbc.co.uk/news/world-south-asia-12641776.

Biersteker, Thomas J. and Sue E. Eckert (2006), "Strengthening Targeted Sanctions Through Fair and Clear Procedures", Watson Institute for International studies, Brown University, available at: http://watsoninstitute.org/pub/Strengthening_Targeted_Sanctions.pdf.

British South Rhodesia (1964-1980), DADM-Project, University of Southern Arkansas Sub-Saharan African Region, available at: http://uca.edu/politicalscience/dadm-project/sub-saharan-africa-region/british-south- rhodesia-1964-1980.

Burki, Shahid Javed (2011), "Pakistan-India Trade", ISAS Brief, National University of Singapore, 211(4).

Chaudhury, Dipanjan Roy (2010), "US Wants India to Act on Iran Sanctions", *Mail Today*, July 15, available at: http://indiatoday.intoday.in/story/us-wants-india-to-act-on-iran-sanctions/1/105461.html.

Chenoy, Anuradha (2013), "India and the Issue of Sanctions", *New Indian Express*, Chennai, April 15.

Choudhury, Upendra (2008), "The Indo-US Nuclear Deal and its Impact on India's Ballistic Missile Programme", South Asian Strategic Stability Institute Research Report 17, June.

Cohen, Stephen (1976), "US Weapons and South Asia: A Policy Analysis", *Pacific Affairs,* 49(1).

Cortright, David and George A. Lopez (2002), "Smart Sanctions: Targeting Economic Statecraft", New York: Rowman & Littlefield.

Crossette, Barbara (1990), "India to Lift Nepal Embargo and Discuss Rift", *New York Times*; July 2, available at: http://www.nytimes.com/1990/06/12/world/india-to-lift-nepal-embargo-and-discuss-rift.html.

Dixit, J.N. (2006), "Indian Foreign Policy: 1947-2003", New Delhi: Thomson Press.

Dixit, Sandeep (2010), "Unilateral Sanctions on Iran will Hurt India", Nirupama Rao" T*he Hindu*, July 6.

Drezner, Daniel W. (1999), "The Sanctions Paradox", Cambridge University Press, Cambridge.

Eagleton, Clyde (1950), "The Case of Hyderabad before the Security

Council", *The American Journal of International Law*, 44(2).

Elliott, Kimberly Ann (2009), "Assessing UN sanctions after the Cold War: New and Evolving Standards of Measurement", *International Journal,* 65(1): 90.

Feiler, Gil (2012), "India's Economic Relations with Israel and the Arabs", *Mideast Security and Policy Studies,* No. 96, The Begin-Sadat Centre for Strategic Studies, available at: http://www.biu.ac.il/SOC/besa/MSPS96.pdf.

Galtung, Johan (1967), "On the Effects of International Economic Sanctions, With Examples from the Case of Rhodesia", *World Politics*, 19(3): 378-416.

Ganguly, Sumit and Manjeet Pardesi (2009), "Explaining Sixty Years of Indian Foreign Policy", *India Review,* 8(5): 4-19.

Garver, John W. (1991), "China-India Rivalry in Nepal: The Clash over Chinese Arms Sales", *Asian Survey,* 31(10).

Grimmett, Jeanne J. (2001), "Nuclear Sanctions: Section 102(b)of the Arms Export Control Act and Its Application to India and Pakistan", CRS Report for Congress, October 5.

Grover, Verinder (1992), "Political Thinkers of Modern India: Rammanohar Lohia", Delhi: Deep and Deep Publications.

Guruswami, Mohan (2008), "There Once was a Hyderabad!" Blogspot, available at: http://mohanguruswamy.blogspot.in.

Gilpin, Robert (1980), "Economic Sanctions as a Response to Terrorism", *Journal of Strategic Studies*, 3: 89-98.

Haass, Richard N. (1997), "Sanctioning Madness", *Foreign Affairs,* 76(6): 74-85.

Hardeep Singh Puri's statement in New York on July 17, 2011, Ministry of External Affairs, available at: http://www.mea.gov.in/SpeechesStatements.htm?dtl/372/Indias+Explanation+of+Vote+after+the+adoption+of+the+tw o+resol utions+succeeding+1267+Sanctions+Regime.

Holum, John D. (1994), "A Revitalized ACDA in the Post-Cold War World", joint hearing before the Subcommittee on International Security, International Organizations, and Human Rights and International Operations of the Committee on Foreign Affairs", House of Representatives, One Hundred Third Congress, second session, June 23, available at: http://archive.org/stream/revitalizedacdai00unit/ revitalizedacdai00unit_djvu.txt.

Hufbauer, Gary et al. (2007), "Economic Sanctions Reconsidered: History and Current Policy", 3rd Edition, Washington D.C.: Peterson Institute of International Economics.

Hufbauer, Gary Clyde (1998), "Sanctions-Happy USA", Institute for International Economics, Policy Brief 98-4, available at: http://www.piie.com/publications/pb/pb.cfm?ResearchID=83.

India News, No. 7/89, Embassy of India, Beijing, March 27, 1989, as quoted in Garver, John W. (1991), "China-India Rivalry in Nepal: The Clash over Chinese Arms Sales", *Asian Survey,* 31(10).

"India Pakistan Relations: 1947-2007", Volume I-X, Public Diplomacy Division, Ministry of External Affairs: CLXXVI.

"India Must Impose Sanctions on Sri Lanka, Tamil Nadu Governor Says", *Times of India*, February 1, available at: http://articles.timesofindia.indiatimes.com/2013-02-01/india/36683386_1_sri-lankan-navy-k-rosaiah-indian-fishermen.

"India, Pakistan Trade Sanctions, Both Say Ready For War", *Space Daily,* December 27, 2001, available at: http://www.spacedaily.com/news/nuclear-india-pakistan-01b.html.

Indian High Commission in South Africa statement, available at: http://www.indiainsouthafrica.com/indiasouthafrica/indiasarelations.html.

"Jaya Calls for Sanctions against Sri Lanka", *The Times of India*, February 21, 2013, available at: http://www.financialexpress.com/news/iran-oil-sanctions-us-exempts-india-china/1201601.

Katzman, Kenneth (2013), "Iran Sanctions", Congress Research Service Report, January 10.

Llyod, Lorna (1991), "A Family Quarrel: The Development of the Dispute over Indians in South Africa", *The Historical Journal*, 34(3): 703-725.

Lohia, Rammanohar (1938), "Indian Foreign Policy", Allahabad: Congress Political and Economic Studies.

Macaskill, Andrew and Jennifer M. Freedman (2012), "UN Rights Council Backs U.S. Demand for New Sri Lanka War Probe", Bloomsberg News, available at: http://www.businessweek.com/news/2012-03-22/un-rights-council-backs-u-dot-s-dot-demand-for-new-sri-lanka-war-probe.

Mohan, Raja C. (2012), "India's New Foreign Policy", Lecture delivered on September 24, 2012 at the Elcano Royal Institute, Madrid, available at:
http://www.realinstitutoelcano.org/wps/portal/rielcano_eng.

Mohan, Raja C. (2010), "Rising India: Partner in Shaping the Global Commons?", *The Washington Quarterly,* 33(3): 133-148.

Mukherji, Rahul (2004), "Economic Sanctions as a Foreign Policy Tool", in Kanti Bajpai and Siddharth Mallavarapu (eds.), 'International Relations in India: Bringing Theory Back Home', New Delhi: Orient Blackswan.

Merom, Jill (2001), "Democracy, Dependency and Destabilization: The Shaking of Alende's Regime", *Political Science Quarterly,* 105(1).

Nehru, Jawaharlal (1966), "India's Foreign Policy: Selected Speeches, September 1946-April 1966", The Publications Division, Ministry of Information and Broadcasting, Government of India. February 19.

Pant, Harsh (2011), "The US-India Nuclear Pact: Policy, Process, and Great Power Politics", Oxford: Oxford University Press.

Pape, Robert A. (1997), "Why Economic Sanctions Do Not Work", *International Security*, 22(2): 90-136.

Pape, Robert (1998), "Why Economic Sanctions Still Do Not Work", *International Security*, 23: 66-77.

Prasad, Bimal (1960), "The Origins of Indian Foreign Policy: The Indian National Congress and World Affairs, 1885-1947", Calcutta: Bookland.

Reilly, James (2012), "China's Unilateral Sanctions", *The Washington Quarterly*, 35(4): 121-133.

Rennack, Dianne E. and Robert D. Shuey (1998), "Economic Sanctions to Achieve U.S. Foreign Policy Goals: Discussion and Guide to Current Law", Washington: Congressional Research Service, Library of Congress.

Routray, Bibhu Prasad (2011), "India-Myanmar Relations: Triumph of Pragmatism", *Jindal Journal of International Affairs*, 1(1): 299-321.

Salman Khurshid's interview "Vietnam Says China Must Avoid Trade Weapon in Maritime Spat" Bloomberg, December 2, 2012, available at:
http://www.bloomberg.com/news/2012-12-02/vietnam-says-china-must-avoid-trade-weapon-in-maritime-disputes.html.

Saran, Shyam (2010), "The Virtue of Pragmatism", *Times of India*, August 7, 2010, available at: http://timesofindia.indiatimes.com/home/opinion/edit-page/The-Virtue-Of Pragmatism/articleshow/6266602.cms.

Spector, Leonard S. (1985), "Silent Spread", *Foreign Policy*, 58: 53-78.

Spector, Leonard S. (2001), "Status of U.S. Sanctions Imposed on India and Pakistan", CNS archive, August 11, available at: http://cns.miis.edu/archive/wtc01/pakind.html.

Statement made by the External Affairs Minister Jaswant Singh, December 27, 2001, Ministry of External Affairs, Government of India, available at: http://www.mea.gov.in/SpeechesStatements.htm?dtl/6024/Text+of+the+Statement+made+by+the+External+Affairs+Minister+Shri+Jaswant+Singh.

Taylor, Brendan (2009), "Sanctions as Grand Strategy", Adelphi Series, 49(411).

The Financial Express (2012), "Iran Oil Sanctions: US Exempts India and China", November 30, available at: http://www.financialexpress.com/news/iran-oil-sanctions-us-exempts-india-china/1201601.

U.N. Doc. S/986, Security Council, Official Records, 3rd Year, Supplementary, September, 1948, available at: http://daccessddsny.un.org/doc/UNDOC/GEN/NL4/809/86/PDF.

United States General Accounting Office Report, "Economic Sanctions: Effectiveness as Tools".

United Nations Security Council Resolution 1696 (2006), Iran, available at: http://www.un.org/ga/search/view_doc.asp?symbol=S/RES/1696%28 2006%29.

United Nations Security Council Resolution 1737 (2006), Non-proliferation, available at: http://www.un.org/ga/search/view_doc.asp?symbol=S/RES /1737% 282006%29.

Unit d Nations Security Council Resolution 216 (1965), Southern Rhodesia, available at: http://daccess-dds-ny.un.org/doc/RESOLUTION/GEN/NR0/222/88/IMG/NR022288.pdf?OpenElement.

Varadarajan, Siddharth (2008), "NSG Lifts Sanctions on India", *The*

Hindu, September 7.

Weiss, Leonard (2007), "US-India Nuclear Cooperation: Better Later than Sooner", *Non-proliferation Review*, 14(3).

7

Political Economy of Decentralization

John S. Moolakkattu and Nisha V. Nair

Introduction

Decentralization has now become a widely accepted strategy for local economic development and democratic deepening all over the world. The World Bank has been contributing to the spread of the idea of decentralization through its study reports and varied forms of development assistance. According to Heller, "Decentralization contributes to democratic deepening if and when it expands the scope and depth of citizen participation in public decision-making. Expanding the depth means incorporating previously marginalized or disadvantaged groups into public politics. Expanding the scope means bringing a wider range of social and economic issues into the authoritative domain of politics (shifting the boundary from the market to the demos)" (Heller, 2001: 140).

Kerala leads all other states in Panchayat Devolution Index (PDI), 2015. In terms of gram panchayat staff, Kerala stands first, and with respect to district panchayat staff also, it is above the national average. Even though Karnataka claims to transfer the largest amount of money to the local bodies in the form of grants, when actual transfer is reckoned, Kerala stands first. In terms of amenities available to the panchayats at all three levels also, Kerala is the frontrunner. So, in terms of all indices, the state's record is quite envious. In 2012, Kerala topped the composite devolution index, by which term the PDI was known then.

The state secured third position in 2013 and second position in 2014. On the functioning of State Finance

Commission, gram sabha and auditing of accounts also, the state has been consistently ranked as the first (PDI, 2015). This demonstrates the robustness of the state's devolution and this status was achieved over a span of just two decades. This paper discusses the distinctive features, gains, problem areas and prospects of decentralization in Kerala taking the last two decades of experience as the reference period. This is done from a largely political economy perspective.

Why Political Economy?

Political economy questions are at the centre of all decentralizing efforts. "Elected officials, political parties, sub-national governments, and key civil society players (such as unions and business associations) act individually and/or in concert in ways that define how decentralization is conceived and implemented. The relative strength of various actors, and the degree to which some of them have common interests, ultimately determine how decentralization evolves—particularly with respect to the initial decision to undertake decentralizing reforms" (Eaton, Kaiser and Smoke, 2010: 16).

The initial decision to devolve substantial funds to the local bodies and enable them to spend money in a participatory mode drawing inputs from the gram sabha was taken by the CPI(M)-led Left Front in 1996, after declaring that the Ninth Five Year Plan of the local bodies will be a 'people's plan'. The structure of the CPI(M) and its adherence to the principle of democratic centralism was seen at odds with decentralization. Even in places like Bengal where panchayat reforms drew national attention, it was the local party that often alternated as the local power structure. Heller thinks that three developments have played a role in the CPI(M)'s fascination with decentralization.

First, it wanted to expand its electoral appeal beyond the state level to the local level at a time of increasing disenchantment with the party's conventional style of

functioning. This also suggested working with local government in an environment in which consensus on questions of development could be formed instead of engaging in confrontation as had been the conventional practice.

Second, there was a realization that the redistributive capacities of the state and its ability to sustain the achievements in the social sector had reached its nadir with the dominant redistributive coalition consisting of employees and workers, which came to capture resources, often standing in the way of further reform. Centralized intervention by the state which had secured all the gains in the social sector was found incapable of meeting the new development challenges, necessitating the need for decentralized governance. Finally, Kerala witnessed by early nineties, a high degree of stagnation in the productive sectors and injecting a new dynamism to revive these sectors was no longer possible through statist intervention (Heller, 2001: 150).

It seems quite clear that only a faction within the CPI(M) close to E.M. Shankaran Namboodiripad (EMS), the de facto party supremo, whose views on decentralization, unlike that of others in the party, were radical, close to the Gandhian tradition rather than Marxian, was instrumental in spearheading the decentralization reform (John, 2007: 22). This avant garde group consisted of members of the State Planning Board and members of the Kerala Sastra Parishad, a pro-CPI(M) movement which had earlier spearheaded the literacy campaign, who worked tirelessly to produce handbooks and other training material as the decentralized planning campaign got under way.

This group provided the epistemic and organizational support to the campaign, which was unprecedented in its scale and operation. The coalition partners were not very enthusiastic about the substantial funds that the decentralization campaign promised to devolve to the local bodies. Their participation as well as those of the local CPI(M) party units and the mass and class organizations associated with the party was minimal. Within the Congress too, the arrival of A.K. Antony as the new Chief Minister in 2001 facilitated the continuation of participatory planning, although short of its voluntary content under a new label known as Kerala Development Programme, despite pressures to reverse the entire process.

The Context

Decentralization in Kerala has assumed a distinct trajectory of its own, which marks it out from the rest of the country in many ways. Kerala had only a single-tier during the pre-amendment phase except for a period of 3 years when the district council experiment was introduced. [1] National level reports did not have much influence in shaping decentralization in the state given the optional nature of their recommendations. The Balwantrai Mehta Committee had suggested a three-tier structure granting the states the option to settle for two tiers should they see it necessary. Only two tiers were contemplated in the state, namely gram panchayat (GP) and district council. Of these two tiers, only the gram panchayats had some kind of an uninterrupted existence, though with erratic elections and occasional supersession by imposing administrative rule.

The Kerala Panchayat Act, 1994, amended in 1999, constitutes the basis of decentralization in modern Kerala. People's planning was seen as a means to carry forward the gains of Kerala model of development in the midst of threats posed by liberalization/globalization and withdrawal of state from the social sector. A very small faction within the CPM under the leadership of EMS provided the inspiration. Although it was organized in a campaign mode in a command style, the rank and file of the party was not intimately involved in it.

Historically, the CPM had no particular strong affinity towards decentralization. Instead, there was preference for state-led and top-down vision of development borrowed largely from the Soviet style planning. But this did not mean that pressures from below had no effect on the polity. Such pressures were seen as creating a congenial setting for state action. Several cases of state action as in the case of land reform and workers' rights were secured through mobilization accompanied by enabling action on the part of a sufficiently capacitated administrative apparatus of the state (Evans, 1995).

Kerala adopted a "big bang" approach to activate the LSGs through participatory planning after creating a working cross-party consensus. It took a bold decision to devolve 35 to 40 percent plan funds to the local bodies with broad sectoral ceilings. Planning was used as a means to strengthen decentralization. The gram sabha was transformed into a source of inputs for planning and selection of beneficiaries. People's planning also was seen as necessary to revive the sagging productive sectors of the state and enhance local economic development. Commentators have variously referred to the decentralization campaign as a case of "synergistic state-society relations" (Heller et al., 2007), and "empowered participatory governance" (Fung and Wright, 2001).

Instead of creating the right legal environment for participatory planning, Kerala decided to use the 1994 Act and simultaneously appointed the Sen Committee to suggest necessary panchayat reforms that could be incorporated through amendments to the Act. It was a process of doing things even as the legal basis for it was created drawing on practice already under way. Kerala has put in place all the institutions mandated by the 73rd Amendment and has even gone beyond. The District Planning Committee (DPC), regular elections every five years, a single appellate tribunal, citizen charters, ombudsman, State Finance Commissions, right to information and local level planning , among others have been institutionalized in the state. However, the unique size of its gram panchayats led it to organize the gram sabha at the ward level. This has created the need to hold the gram sabha spread over at least a week since the Sabhas have to be presided over by the president or, in his/her absence, by the vice-president.

Some Features of Decentralization in Kerala

Half of all seats in all local bodies and half of all positions are reserved for women in Kerala. While the 73rd Amendment had mandated only 33 percent reservation, Kerala raised it to 50 percent from the 2010 election onwards and subsequently made the quota applicable to all positions including the DPC. Inter-tier relations are not hierarchical in Kerala. Thus, the district panchayat, block panchayat and gram panchayat function autonomously. Coordination among the tiers is effected through a process of co-responsibility. MLAs and MPs have only minimal roles in the panchayat set up except as invitees in DPCs and gram sabhas. Bureaucratic domination, though present, is not overbearing. Kerala also has the most visible GPs anywhere in India, so also the busiest elected members at that level. The block and district panchayats do not have own resources and they are almost wholly dependent on grants from the state. A support structure of women in the form of Kudumbasree SHGs is available in the GPs. This support structure ensures that all projects for poverty alleviation as well as for women are carried out through its intermediation. The SHGs ensure the necessary quorum for meetings of the gram sabha.

Less space for elite capture is available at the local level in Kerala due to the intermediary role of political parties and the overall pro-poor tone of panchayat plans with the exception of investments in the infrastructure sector. Over the years, there has been a marked shift from focus on the productive sector to the service and infrastructure sectors. Most of the individual-based projects in the service sectors benefit the poorer sections. The Gram Sabhas are not thronged by the rich and the powerful. Instead, women associated with the SHGs, people who are expecting benefits (particularly those belonging to the below poverty line category) and a few supporters of the elected member of the ward are ordinarily present in the Sabha. There is no space for deliberation or participation in the capacity of a citizen. The Kerala Panchayat Raj Act says that citizens are entitled to discuss the administrative report of the panchayat relating to the previous year. But this does not happen anywhere.

Kerala has a functional local government ombudsman, a quasi-judicial body to check malpractices in local governments in the discharge of developmental functions headed by a retired High Court Judge. Further, it has put into effect the right to information provisions at the level of the local bodies much before they were made at the national and state levels. In addition, the Panchayat Act talks about citizen charters. Some panchayats have published such charters. Elections to local bodies are contested along political lines. A miniature form of state level coalitions exists in most panchayats, although occasional breaches are not uncommon. Many smaller parties that have no representation in the legislative assembly are able to find representation in local bodies.

Decentralization in Kerala has weathered changes in government and there is no possibility of reversal of the advances by future governments. No radical changes in the institutional structure took place even during the most vulnerable phase of 2001-2002. This was a time when the participatory planning experiment was criticized from a radical faction within the CPI(M) as a neo-liberal project of the West disguised in a participatory mode. Many in the new government were keen to reverse the process, considering the difficulties the devolution of substantial funds to the local bodies caused to the financial health of the state. However, A.K. Antony, the then Chief Minister, played a key role in ensuring that the funds transferred to local bodies was not curtailed, despite the austerity measures the state took to tide over the financial crisis.

Some Dysfunctional Features

There is a structural discrepancy between the panchayat

seen as the unit of planning and the electoral ward where accountability is located. This has led to fragmentation and suboptimal use of funds losing advantages of economies of scale. There is also considerable lack of capacity to spend funds. Further, plans are all in the form of disjointed wish lists without any long-term perspective. There are also coordination problems with higher levels such as block panchayat and district panchayat. This is most pronounced when different parties are in power at different levels. The block panchayat plans and gram panchayat plans are formulated independently of each other with individual beneficiary schemes targeted at the same set of beneficiaries (Government of Kerala, 2009: 272).

There is also lack of cooperation between old president and the new president—even if they both belong to the same party. The existing women's quota system relies on single member wards with the ward de-reserved in the next round of elections. This does not provide enough incentives to the elected member, be it a woman under the quota system or a man under the general category. The recent study by the State Planning Board also suggests that the current division of resources (especially plan funds) between the elected representatives may be discouraged and the gram panchayat and not the electoral ward should be treated as the unit of development.

The study also suggested that a minimum level of expenditure may be stipulated in each quarter of the plan year considering the fact that planning is not a whole-year effort even now (Government of Kerala, 2016b). There is something like a plan holiday in the first two quarters and a rush of expenditure towards the end of the year. Enhancement of women's quota to 50 percent has not led to changed priorities, changed style in politics, or more women in leadership positions in the party. Women component plan, a form of pre-gender responsive budgeting introduced at the local level that entails allocation of ten percent of the plan funds of each local body, has now become a preserve of the Kudumbasree units (Nair and Moolakkattu, 2014).

The focus hitherto has been on annual planning for development. This has impacted on the civic functions of the GPs, particularly functions like waste disposal and services to be provided by the panchayat office. There is an absence of a concept of local economic development. Local development that carries the distinct qualities of the locality is absent. There is uniformity instead of diversity everywhere—in projects and practices. The tendency to imitate is more widespread than innovate. This is partly due to the command style in which the original campaign was initiated and the numerous orders, often conflicting, issued by the panchayat department from time to time. Given the nature of the landscape and settlement pattern, scope for inter-panchayat cooperation and joint projects is high. However, there is very little cooperation of that kind. There has also been a progressive decline in the expenditure on productive sectors contrary to the expectations of the initiators of the decentralized plan campaign. Finally, there is no continuity between the budget and the plan at the local government level. Unlike the panchayat plan, the budget remains a largely unrealistic exercise, to fulfill a statutory requirement. Failure to present the budget will invite dismissal of the panchayat concerned.

There has been some kind of exhaustion of innovative ideas on decentralization both on the part of left and the right even after 20 years of decentralization reforms. Old ideas are merely rehashed. Focus on plan fund utilization year after year has led to less attention on civic and core functions such as waste disposal, service delivery and office management. Most GPs can improve own resources considerably if they really decide to do so given the wide gap between the potential sources of revenue and the actual collection. Multi-member constituencies and direct election of president are options that can take decentralization forward in the state and also address the resentment caused by reservation of seats for women in alternative terms. But such suggestions are not considered favourably by the political parties.

Although gram sabhas are held routinely, the forum is not able to attract a cross-section of society. The middle classes, salaried classes and the upper castes generally tend to shy away from the gram sabha. They use alternative routes for accessing the resources of the panchayat. This makes the participatory base of participatory planning very narrow. In the early stages of the campaign, the gram sabha was divided into different groups and sectoral discussions were common. This has given way to a kind of mechanical participation to fulfil the statutory requirement with quorums often manufactured (Moolakkattu and Nair, 2014). Civil society activism on the decentralization front is also weak in Kerala. Williams and Thampy (2013) hold the view that moving the state to the local area has not always led to the inclusion of certain groups. Drawing on data from Wayanad and Palghat district, their study concludes that even at the gram panchayat level, several minority groups get excluded in what they call "new micro-geographies of exclusion" (Williams and Thampi, 2013).

Greater Expenditure Autonomy

During the Twelfth Five Year Plan, a number of progressive developments that enhanced the autonomy in expenditure decisions of the panchayats took place. There is now no mandatory minimum or maximum ceiling in productive or service sectors. In order to prevent infrastructure sector from cornering all funds, a ceiling was fixed with 45 percent as the maximum for gram panchayats and block panchayats, 55 percent for municipalities and corporations and 50 percent for district panchayats in General Sector Plan Outlay. There has not been any change in the 10 percent of the development fund earmarked for Women Component Plan. Over the years, an additional 5 percent has been earmarked for children, old age groups, differently-abled, palliative care and other vulnerable segments. This represents a marked shift in interpreting the marginalized groups in a more expansive manner. The Annual Plan Document of local bodies needs to be approved by the District Planning Committee (DPC) and not individual projects as was the earlier practice (Government of Kerala, 2012; Government of Kerala, 2016a).

How do elected women perform in decentralized governance in Kerala? Devika and Thampi (2012) opine that the older discourse on rights has given way to one based on welfare benefits wherein some kind of "feminine public altruism" rules the roost. Instead of changing the idioms of politics, women presidents see their power to be used as "altruistic agents of welfare disbursal" in a traditional feminine mould. Without being apolitical in the true sense of the term, they tend to project local space as apolitical, taking into account the barriers faced by them in terms of finances, past experience, family and political party support. Chathukulam and John (2000) referred to it as 'panchayat feminism' which has no potential to expand the political space for women.

Fiscal Decentralization

The fiscal part of decentralization constitutes in many ways the most significant facet of Kerala's decentralization. The Fourth SFC Commission recommended that at least 25 percent of the likely Plan size should be devolved to LGs for development purpose. The fund would be inclusive of the devolution from the 13th Finance Commission and the amount flowing to LGs from the proposed World Bank supported project namely, 'Kerala Local Government Service Delivery Project'. However, under no circumstances should any year's allocation be less than 25 percent of Plan size for that year. The recommended allocation to local self-governments by the Fourth State Finance Commission and actual allocation done so far is given in Table 7.1 (Government of Kerala 2016a: 350). It may be noted that, by 2015-16, this was to reach a share of 30 percent through annual increases. This did not happen.

Table 7.1 shows that the quantum of devolution has more or less settled around 25 percent of the state's Plan size, which is considerably lower than the 35 percent promised when the decentralized planning experiment was initiated in 1996. Until the recommendations of the Fourth State Finance Commission, this amount was exclusive of the Central Finance Commission award. Hence, in real terms, the quantum of funds devolved would be still lower than 25 percent.

Table 7.1: Development Fund for LGs (2011-16)

Year	SFC recommended amount (₹ crore)	Actual allocation (₹ crore)	Percentage of total state plan outlay
2011-12	2,750	2,750	25
2012-13	3,388	3,228	23
2013-14	3,933	4,000	24
2014-15	4,559	4,700	24
2015-16	5,193	4,800	24

Strengthening Participatory Planning

Heller says that three technical/organizational aspects need to work if local government reform is to succeed. First, any successful planning process requires certain technical inputs. Data must be gathered, plans drawn up, and budgets made. Second is the problem of coordination between levels and the provision of public goods. Not all governance functions can be decentralized. The provision of public goods requires central authority and capacity. Successful planning must be integrated. This calls for effective and constant coordination between levels of government. Decentralization thus requires building a delicate balance of division of authority and competence between levels while creating structures and avenues for coordination. Third, democracy requires bureaucracy. Because participation can never be comprehensive or continuous (capacities for participation are uneven and cannot be sustained throughout the planning and implementation process), there is a need to routinize and formalize the process through which participatory inputs are translated into outputs; hence, the technical requirement for rules of transparency, accountability, representation, and decisional authority" (Heller, 2001: 136).

The vaunted participatory methodology has lost much of its élan. The process of planning starting from the gram sabha is a sound one, but over years, it has become routinized with very little participatory content in terms of public input into the planning process. Local level planning always had a very short time span, restricted to annual plans. There was no perspective planning. There was also no district plan worth the name, and none of the DPCs has attempted to prepare one so far. Not much progress could be made on the service delivery front or in the participatory monitoring of projects.

Although several attempts have been made to revitalize the gram sabha, nothing has come of it. The 2009 Evaluation Committee recommended that "GS meetings may be reduced to two and the quorum be reduced to 5 percent" (Government of Kerala, 2009: 259). At present, it is expected to meet four times a year. However, two meetings alone are mandatorily held in all panchayats, one before the finalization of annual plan and one during the plan implementation stage. The Evaluation Committee felt that it was better to have 5 percent of the total membership drawn from a cross-section of society as the quorum than ten percent of the membership with poor women constituting the majority of the attendees.

However, the fact of the matter is that the elected representatives themselves are wary of participation by the engaged sections. They generally do not favour a vibrant deliberative body and are happy with the present women-dominated sabhas with a sprinkling of party supporters. Heller et al. (2007) say, that when it comes to the question of gram sabha participation in an inegalitarian society, we need to be attentive of the "depth of participation" or "the magnitude and social composition of participation", "the quality of participation" or "the extent to which the participatory process approximates a deliberative process that involves substantive public discussions and efforts to identify common interests" and the "process dimension of participation" or "the extent to which participatory inputs find their way through institutions and are translated into actual outputs" (Heller et al., 2007: 631-632).

Conclusion

Kerala has institutionalized a unique form of decentralization reforms brought into effect through a campaign mode. Decentralization in Kerala has become synonymous with participatory planning, which has now dissipated into planning done by a few individuals. Although gram sabha is consulted for GP plans, it does not effectively exercise any sway over the planning process. At best, the participants may ask what projects are proposed for the ward concerned and nothing more. Focus on planning has affected the civic functions and toning up of office management procedures. Only 11.65 percent of the total receipts of the GPs come from own revenue (PDI, 2015: 100), which can be improved considerably given the potential that exists. Reduced dependence on grants implies greater autonomy.

Tax diversification has not been fully exploited in the state by the GPs with nearly 95 percent of the revenues coming from property tax and profession tax. Substantial sums of money are to reach the GPs in the coming years in the form of the Fourteenth Finance Commission award for performance of their mandatory functions. Panchayat institutions in Kerala are in a better position compared to the rest of the country in terms of functions, funds, and functionaries. They have experience of handling several crores of rupees annually.

What Kerala is addressing now are second generation problems. This requires a qualitative change in the way leadership is constituted at the local level or a total change in the lens of local governance. Direct election of the president at the GP level and the introduction of some form of a proportional representation with multi-member constituencies are some of the means to tone up the administration, improve planning procedures and enhance the status of the local bodies. However, this requires support from the state level political leaders who are generally wary of enhancing the status of the local bodies since they see any such change in zero sum terms.

Note

1. The District Administration Act, which was initially mooted in late fifties, was actually passed in 1979 when A.K. Antony of the Congress party was the Chief Minister. However, it had to wait for another 12 more years to be put into practice. The Karunakaran ministry that came to power in 1982 kept it in cold storage. The Nayanar government that came to power in 1987 took a year to appoint a special advisor to submit a report to the government on democratic decentralization. Although the report was submitted in three months, it took another 20 months to finalise the elections to the district council (DC). The four years that Nayanar government took to implement it suggests that both the fronts are no better as far as commitment to decentralization is concerned. The amendments made in the 1979 Act on the advice of the special advisor did not actually change the earlier act much except removal of the ex-officio membership of MLAs and the periodicity of appointment of the Finance Commission from 3 years to 5 years. The advisor was not in favour of the DC controlling the gram panchayats and wanted a greater role for the DC in the preparation of the district plan both of which were not accepted by the government. The Karunakaran government that came to power in 1991 amended it and made the DC a mere cipher, liberally granting ex-officio membership to MLAs and MPs, often in more than one DC if their constituency fell under two districts. This increase in membership led to reduction in the weight of women in the council. Besides taking back the powers, the collector who was the secretary was replaced by a person of the rank of deputy collector (EPW Commentary, 1991).

References

Chathukulam, Jos and M.S. John (2002), "Five Years of Participatory Planning in Kerala: Rhetoric and Reality",

Economic and Political Weekly, Vol. 37, No. 49, December 7-13, 4917-4926.

Chathukulam, Jos and M.S. John (2000), "Empowerment of Women Panchayat Members: Learning from Kerala", *Asian Journal of Women's Studies*, Vol. 6, No. 4, 66-101.

Devika, J. and B.V. Thampi (2012), "New Lamps for Old? Gender Paradoxes of Political Decentralization in Kerala", New Delhi: Zubaan.

EPW Commentary (1991), "Debasement of District Councils in Kerala", *Economic and Political Weekly*, Vol. 26, No. 49, 2793-2795.

Evans, Peter B. (1995), "Embedded Autonomy: States and Industrial Transformation", Princeton: Princeton University Press.

Fung, A. and E.O. Wright (2001), "Deepening Democracy: Innovations in Empowered Participatory Governance", *Politics and Society*, Vol. 29, No. 1, 5-41.

Government of Kerala (2009), "Report of the Committee for Evaluation of Decentralised Planning and Development, Trivandrum", available at:
http://www.lsgkerala.gov.in/htm/PDF/report_decentralised_plannin g.pdf.

Government of Kerala (2013), "Economic Review, 2012", Trivandrum: Kerala State Planning Board.

Government of Kerala (2016a), "Economic Review, 2015", Trivandrum: Kerala State Planning Board.

Government of Kerala (2016b), "Report on Performance Assessment of Grama Panchayats under Decentralised Planning", State Planning Board Trivandrum, available at:
http://www.spb.kerala.gov.in/images/pdf/Divisions/DPD/SR%2 0DPD.pdf.

Heller, Patrick (2001), "Moving the State: The Politics of Democratic Decentralization in Kerala, South Africa, and Porto Alegre", *Politics and Society*, Vol. 29, No. 1, 131-163.

Heller, Patrick, K.N. Harilal and Shubham Chaudhuri (2007), "Building Local Democracy: Evaluating the Impact of Decentralization in Kerala, India", *World Development*, Vol. 35, No. 4, 626-648.

John, M.S. (2007), "Gandhi and the Contemporary Discourse on Decentralisation" in T.M. Joseph (ed.), 'Local Governance in India: Ideas, Challenges and Strategies', New Delhi: Concept

Publishers.

Moolakkattu, John S. and Nisha V. Nair (2014), "Women's Participation in the Gram Sabha: Some Observations from a Micro Setting in Kerala", *Madhya Bharti,* University Research Journal of Dr. Harisingh Gour Central University, Sagar, Vol. 65, No. 2.

Moolakkattu, John S. and Jos, Chathukulam (2007), "Between Euphoria and Scepticism: Ten Years of Panchayati Raj in Kerala" in M.A. Oommen (ed.), 'A Decade of Decentralisation in Kerala: Experience and Lessons', New Delhi: Har-Anand.

Nair, Nisha V. and John S. Moolakkattu (2014), "Women Component Plan at the Local Level in Kerala: Does it Live up to its Promise?", *Indian Journal of Gender Studies*, Vol. 21, No. 2, 247-276.

"Panchayat Devolution Index, 2015", available at: http://devolutionlsg.in/properties/pdf/Other%20important%20findings.pdf.

Williams, G.O. and B.V. Thampi (2013), "Decentralisation and the Changing Geographies of Political Marginalisation in Kerala", *Environment and Planning: An International Journal of Urban and Regional Research*, Vol. 45, No. 6, 1337-1357.

8

Knowledge Management in Higher Education

C. Beena

Education, or more specifically, higher education, is the way to empowerment of people and the development of nations. Knowledge generation has replaced ownership of capital assets and labour productivity as the source of growth and prosperity. Innovation is seen as the mantra for development. Knowledge creation requires a network of scholars actively engaged in its pursuit because the search for the unknown is a product of engaged minds, constantly challenging the known in an enabling environment. The modern university is the ideal space for the ecosystem of scholars to search for new ideas in a spirit of free inquiry.

Knowledge management is the process of capturing and making use of organization's expertise and experience wherever it resides and distribute it wherever needed.

Higher Education

Higher education in India is passing through a phase of paradigm shift by extraordinary expansion marked by an explosion in the volume of students, a substantial expansion in the number of institutions and quantum jump in the level of public funding. Higher education covers diversified fields of education and research in different disciplines. Higher education must include mastery of more than one language and ability to communicate effectively in those languages. Higher education sector is creating information and applying this information and producing new knowledge. This knowledge to be shared with the public requires advanced ICT infrastructure, a vibrant repository and an open access to technologies.

Universities produce the bulk of original research—both basic and applied, in most countries—and receive the most funding for research. Their professors are hired on the basis of their qualifications to conduct research and are rewarded for research prowess and productivity. The academic culture of these universities focuses on research. In the hierarchy of academic values, research ranks highest, although teaching and advisory services remain important. Most of the academic community, including the undergraduate students, often have the opportunity to participate in research and are exposed to the research culture.

The Knowledge

Knowledge can be defined as the facts, information and skills acquired through experience or education; the theoretical or practical understanding of the subject (Oxford dictionary). Knowledge is of two types: explicit Knowledge (can be written down, transferred and shared and can be protected by the legal system); and tacit knowledge (know-how and is by nature difficult to describe).

Explicit knowledge, which can be expressed in words and numbers, can be easily communicated and shared in hard form, as scientific formulas, codified procedures, or universal principles. Tacit or unarticulated knowledge is more personal, experiential, context specific, and hard to formalize. This kind of knowledge is difficult to communicate or share with others, and is generally known only to an individual or a team. It can be demonstrated but rarely codified, and resides with its holder. Since knowledge may be an organization's only sustainable competitive advantage, it is very important to capture tacit knowledge.

Knowledge Management

Knowledge does not have any boundaries, either space or time and the process of knowledge growth is evergreen and everlasting. It is multi-nuclear, multi-focussed, globally multiplicative and multi-faceted. Every individual on earth acquires knowledge and also generates it; collective generation of knowledge leads the beginning of knowledge society. The exponential growth of knowledge is due to the intellectuals who started contributing knowledge in different domains and in different formats. Proper management of this knowledge is the only solution for an effective utilization of this knowledge.

Knowledge management is not a new concept. Since times immemorial, human beings have been searching for new ideas and concepts for the livelihood from their experience and creating knowledge from these ideas, concepts and lessons learned through experience, they preserved and shared this knowledge for the next generation—this knowledge is called tacit knowledge. It is the innovation and creativity, which is rooted in every normal human being that helps him or her in solving some daily and challenging problems. The development of knowledge management in recent years has become a key concern for many organizations in the business world and in higher education sector also.

Educational institutions are considered as "knowledge houses" where knowledge flows from academia and R&D labs to scholars etc. and new knowledge is created. Hence, in the academic system, especially in higher education sector, knowledge management system is necessary to record the generated knowledge. Undoubtedly, knowledge is a significant contributor to an organization's success in a modern economy. Due to this fact, many organizations showcase or manage their intellectual capital in a scientific way.

Knowledge Management in Higher Education

Educational institutions, especially higher education sector, is the knowledge producing centre as it involves the creation of knowledge, its dissemination and the subsequent learning. Knowledge management is an emerging and essential field in the academic environment. Many international and national institutions are actively engaged in knowledge management research.

Knowledge of an organization does not reside in a structured form of information and data. The discovery of such knowledge is a difficult task as the characteristic is dynamic, scattered, massive and multiplying at high speed. Conventional methods of managing scattered information are too resource demanding and time consuming to cope with the rapid information growth. Knowledge management is a fast growing process in any academic or industrial organization. It is one of the key components of an organization's objectives such as improved performance, competitive advantage, innovation, the sharing of lessons learnt and integration of its national and global level operations for its continuous improvement. Knowledge management is a process where organizations have formulated ways in an attempt to identify and archive intellectual informatics within the organization, even from other organizations that share the similar area of interest or specialization (Bouthiller and Shearer, 2002). In this context, an institution wide approach to knowledge management can largely facilitate sharing process both explicit and tacit.

Organizational Culture

Organizational culture is the collective behaviour of humans who are a part of an organization and the meanings that the people attach to their actions. Culture includes the organization's values, visions, norms, working language, systems, symbols, beliefs and habits. It is also the pattern of such collective behaviours and assumptions that are taught to new organizational members as a way of perceiving, and even thinking and feeling. Organizational culture affects the way people and groups interact with each other, with clients, and with stakeholders (Wikipedia).

The ability of any organization to adapt effectively is influenced by its culture. The basic definition of organizational culture is "the way we do things around here" and it is easy to recognize that things are done differently in different organizations. Organizational culture describes the collective perceptions, beliefs and values of employees in the workplace. Organizational culture enables core values, infrastructure, rules and values, interaction within the organization and team spirit. The core values include collaboration and communication within the campus and at the national and international level, interaction, innovation, adoption, learning, orientation etc. Academic infrastructure means transparent decision-making, information access and sharing, communication channels, infrastructure for information preservation, sharing, accessing etc.

Open Access

Open access (OA) means that a reader of a scientific publication can read it over the intemet, print it or download it. Budapest Open Access Initiative (BOAI) defines open access as: "free availability on the internet, permitting any users to read, download, copy, distribute and/or print, with the possibility to search or link to the full texts of these articles, crawl them for indexing, pass them as data to software, or use them for any other lawful purpose, without financial, legal, or technical barriers other than those inseparable from gaining access to the internet itself and even further distribute it for non-commercial purposes without any payments or restrictions".

Open access movement and open source software has given high relevance in the area of knowledge management practice in educational, business, corporate and industrial sector. Open access supports in higher education results in access to huge volumes of scholarly communications made available at the open platform for free access. Open software solutions help many information professionals to develop cost effective solutions for managing the organizational knowledge.

Scholarly Communication

Universities and R&D institutions produce large volume of research output in the form of research publications, theses, dissertations, and project reports.

Scholarly communication can be defined as "the system

through which research and other scholarly writings are created, evaluated for quality, disseminated to the scholarly community, and preserved for future use. The system includes both formal means of communication, such as publication in peer-reviewed journals, and informal channels, such as electronic leisters". In an environment that is increasingly global, many scholarly communication programmes encourage the advancement of effective, extensible, sustainable, and economically viable models of scholarly communication that provide barrier-free access to quality information (Wikipedia). Open access journals support free flow of scholarly outcomes and also comprises of creation, exchange, dissemination, evaluation, registration, and archiving of the outcomes of research and other scholarly activities. It also supports the multidisciplinary research and cognition.

Globalization

Globalization is both a benefit and a curse to research universities (Knight, 2008; Marginson and van der Wende, 2009b). Research universities are at the centre of global knowledge communication and networks. They funnel new ideas and knowledge into the higher education system and the country as well. In the age of internet, individuals anywhere can take advantage of global knowledge, but the resources and academic community of research universities make international participation easier and more effective. In many countries, research universities may be the only institutions adequately linked to global networks. Thus, research universities provide a two-way street for scientific participation. At the same time, for many universities globalization constitutes a challenge. The global academic marketplace for professors and students means that the best students and staff members can be enticed away. Over-reliance on international core journals for promotion and research criteria may place professors in peripheral research universities at a disadvantage. Globalization tends to favour universities at the centre over others; it does not necessarily contribute to the democratization of science and scholarship.

Knowledge Management Models and Life Cycle

Knowledge management system is defined as the process to manage knowledge in an organization from identification, validation, creation, acquisition, codification, sharing, and measurement of knowledge impact and creation of intellectual outcomes.

There are four basic KM models that have been selected based on the ability to meet the growing global demands of an organization. The four models are the Zack, from Meyer and Zack (1996), the Bukowitz and Williams (2000), the McElroy (2003), and the Wiig (1993) KM cycles. In all these 4 models of KM, the main premise is of acquisition of knowledge, processing of knowledge, storing or preservation and finally the distribution or sharing of knowledge.

Knowledge management life cycle is a practice of transforming the information generated by the institution from personal experience, education and training, intelligent sources, media, books and peer groups etc. into knowledge within the organization. It explains how knowledge is captured, processed or managed and distributed in an organization.

In KM lifecycle, scholars identify research problems and the available data from a senior's work and the literature survey. From their work, they derive some new concepts and ideas that can be communicated as research publications or research literature. Again, this can be used by other scholars or students who are working in a similar area. Final research reports or theses should be available at the global level through institutional repository which can again be used subsequently by another scholar for their research work.

How are the Universities Applying KM Models?

Almost all universities or institutions in higher education sector have started a strategy for managing the intellectual outcomes of an institution. One of the best examples for such initiative is the national repository of electronic theses and dissertation sponsored by UGC-INFLIBNET. Indian Council of Agricultural Research (ICAR) has been showcasing all the agricultural research outcomes in their own repository. Almost all ministries of Government of India have also initiated such knowledge management models. CSIR started the traditional knowledge digital library (TKDL) for herbal medicine. Many research laboratories in India have started consortia for sharing their research outcomes as for example, DRDO labs, Central Marine Fisheries Research Institutions (CMFRI) etc.

Here, one needs to mention one of the cost effective models of knowledge management developed by Cochin University of Science and Technology (CUSAT) for promoting innovation and interdisciplinary research at the global level. CUSAT research theses are available in the digital repository of CUSAT called "dyuthi" at dyuthi.cusat.ac.in. It covers conference proceedings, pre-prints and post-prints of research articles etc. Bibliographical details of research publications are organized in "YUJ" available at yuj.cusat.ac.in. It covers the research publications of CUSAT, 'pen names" of the authors, national and international collaborations of the authors, citation index etc.

CUSAT learning resources such as books, journals, e-books etc. are managed by open source software termed as KOHA. It is available at opac.library.ac.in. All the department resources are coordinated in a union catalogue and are available at unioncatlogue.cusat.ac.in.

Events happened at CUSAT are showcased at media.cusat.ac.in. It is a video repository of Cochin University of Science and Technology and covers educational, recreational, featured videos of events at CUSAT as well as created by the CUSAT community.

This knowledge management model of CUSAT supports the collaborative learning and sharing of research outcomes at the international level. It also provides visibility of the students and faculty at the global level and supports new innovations and competencies in the areas of science, social science and technology.

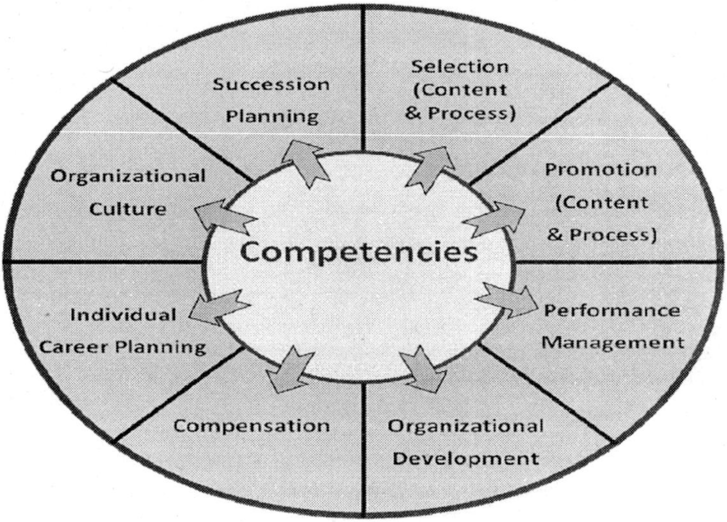

Future of Knowledge Management in Higher Education

Future perspectives of knowledge management are superfluous because knowledge management is an essential, inseparable ingredient and integral to all activities whether it is higher education or the corporate sector. Future's big issue is how well they generate the right type of knowledge and how well they manage the same for competitive global advantage. Today, students are digital natives. Future of knowledge and information would be in e-format. Knowledge identification, acquisition, taxonomy, access and sharing etc. will be in complete e-form or through smart phones and smart electronic gadgets. Visuals will replace the text-based list.

Future social networks and social media will blend with knowledge management solutions or software and resultantly the communication and collaboration within an organization or among the peers will be easy. Social media and linked knowledge will provide an easy way to capture and reuse knowledge. It will help in addressing the research problems, supporting content creation, collaboration and sharing of important social insights. More than that, it will help in provide the right knowledge to right people at the right time.

Conclusion

This paper explores some important aspects of knowledge management in higher educational institutions. Knowledge and knowledge management have become a vital concern for organizations in recent years since it offers lot of fundamental benefits including innovations, interdisciplinary research and competences, ranking of the organizations etc. Development of information and communication technology (ICT) has given an enormous scope for developing knowledge management strategies in organizations. Without knowledge management, existence of an organization especially in higher education sector is difficult. The core stages of KM in organizations is identifying, storing, integrating, processing, generating distributing and exploiting the same in a continuous fashion. There are many national level initiatives taking place in this regard. Many developing countries have also initiated such knowledge management practices.

References

Beena, C., P.K. Padmakumar and S.N. Archana (2013), "Knowledge Management: Creating Competitive Intelligence for the Future", 9th International CALIBER, 2013, INFLIBNET Centre, Gandhinagar, Gujarat, March 21-23.

Bouthillier, F. and K. Shearer (2002), "Understanding Knowledge Management and Information Management: The Need for an Empirical Perspective", Information Research, 8(1), paper no. 141, available at: http://InformationR.net/ir/8-1/paper141.html.

Jawad, Kayani and M. Qamar Zia (2012), "The Analysis of Knowledge, Knowledge Management and Knowledge Management Cycles: A Broad Review", *International Journal of*

Academic Research in Economics and Management Sciences, Vol. 1, No. 6, 152-162.

McElroy, M.W. (2003), "The New Knowledge Management: Complexity, Learning and Sustainable Innovation", KMCI Press.

Meyer, M., and M. Zack (1996), "The Design and Implementation of Information Products", *Sloan Management Review*, 37(3), 43-59.

Wiig, K. (1993), "Knowledge Management Foundations", Arlington, TX: Schema Press.

9

Electronic and Digital Learning Possibilities in India

Sajimon Abraham

Introduction

Education plays an important role in ensuring the economic growth of a country. At present, the teaching learning process is undergoing revolutionary changes and the students are becoming more and more technology oriented.

In this changing environment, it is important to think about the latest technologies to be incorporated into the teaching and learning process. Integration of new technologies in the field of education offers new challenges and opportunities in e-learning. E-learning is powerful, because it allows individuals to learn 'anywhere, anytime' and gives instant access to specific knowledge. E-learning can include training, the delivery of just-in-time information and guidance from experts.

Prime Minister Narendra Modi's vision and efforts for Digital India are being well-received by the Silicon Valley in the US. While it means a lot for Indians the way they live and work, it would also give a new meaning to the country's education sector. A recent UK-India Business Council report titled, "Meeting India's Educational Challenges Through E-Learning" states that India is the second biggest e-learning market globally after the US.

Digital India Campaign

These days the country's education sector is undergoing a revolution, thanks to the rapid internet penetration and the availability of low-cost mobile and hand-held devices. Since technology is playing a major role in multiplying reach and providing access to learning tools and material, this opportunity is being seen as a huge potential by many foreign and domestic training providers offering online education opportunities in the country. "Yet efforts are still fragmented and many of the more advanced innovations in online education technology remain the remit of private enterprises. In an effort to bring rural India into the digital age, the Centre has launched the Digital India campaign. Some of this campaign's targets include providing broadband connectivity to a quarter of a million rural villages by 2019 and making wi-fi connections available in schools", says the report.

How to Reach the Learners?

So how is this impacting e-learning and digital education providers? According to Atul Kulshrestha, chairman and managing director, Extra Marks, "Digital education today is no longer limited to the four walls of a classroom. It has paved way for virtual classrooms, making learning attainable and providing easy access everywhere and every time. This has allowed students to use digital learning as a 'flipped classroom' adding considerable value to the manner in which education is imparted.

The latest trends in digital education space also include adaptive and collaborative learning where a student is engaged by practicing, experiencing, sharing things and gaining knowledge in a collaborative environment. The fourth generation of communication technology is speculated to revolutionize the digital education space by providing cutting-edge user experience".

Another digital learning provider McGraw Hill Education India is also making efforts to provide access to learning material and tools to learners. "Our aim is to use educational technology to help students and teachers learn and teach better. Studies have shown that technologies enable personalised learning yielda for better outcomes. Through online learning and multimedia tools, students of all ages, teachers and professionals are engaged, stimulated and empowered to succeed with tools like SmartBooks, Learnsmart, Access Science and Access Engineering", opines Kaushik Bellani, M.D., McGraw Hill Education India.

Giving examples on the ways digital learning is reaching students, Kulshrestha says, "A talk-n-chalk classroom is being replaced by an interactive whiteboard with projectors and speakers, which is student centric that breeds immersive learning environment. Reports show that a number of institutions are taking steps to adopt the digital approach towards learning. The changed perspective is evident from the fact that all good schools have now switched to Smart Learn Classes as per the current trend.

They are no longer rigid in their teaching methodologies. To support e-learning, students require easy availability of mobile devices like tablets and smartphones, to make the flipped class a reality. We need to spread more awareness amongst the teaching fraternity, students and most importantly parents about the marvels of the digital education space. We have recently launched a pay per use app aimed at making learning by engaging through digital learning solutions which include rich multimedia and animations to make learning easy and effective.

These learning solutions cover entire CBSE and ICSE board and offer various study options to students like Quick Study and Just a Minute which present a synopsis of the entire lesson in a single view. It also offers high order thinking skills questions, virtual lab experiments, solved Board papers, formative discussions, chapter-wise Q&A to substantiate learning with practice. It also contains MCQs and quizzes to let students assess themselves at each level for strong understanding about the subject matter. The real time progress can be tracked and a performance report is instantly generated".

Impact Factors

For digital learning to make an impact till the last mile, there has to be a larger vision of integrating technology into our complex education system. To achieve this, it is imperative that we put our stakes on digital infrastructure, ready access, quality e-content and affordability. Learning should be made interactive and fun for the learners to exponentially enhance retention and application, adds Bellani.

The government's focus is to integrate technology in digital learning for both urban and rural India. It is also looking at public-private-partnerships to enhance reach in rural and remote areas.

To have a positive impact on learning and solve big educational problems in India, technology is not the only solution that we are looking at. There is need to have a bigger vision of enabling technology to help students learn better and teachers teach better. Therefore, solutions to hurdles like affordability, accessibility, mode of delivery and content are indispensable.

Technology has made it possible to implement digital classrooms. "Through technology, efficiencies and transparency can be brought into schools by helping stakeholders such as students, teachers, parents and administrators streamline routine tasks, improve assessments and learner/teacher data collection. However, the greatest advantage of using technology in classrooms remains the uniformity of the educational process which ensures that the same quality of education is delivered in all domains and regions, and also improves the efficiency of the teachers' manifolds", says Kulshrestha.

Experts also believe that for inputs to be translated into learning, it is important that the learning is interactive besides being digital. "The digital education space is at a nascent stage in India.

The industry is fragmented and there is no player currently who is offering a suite of courses to cater to the varied needs of learners. Since, e-learning is at a buoyant stage, live interactivity that empowers high engagement and social collaborative learning has rendered the conventional format of e-learning led by recorded lectures and course slightly inadequate. Digital learning as a format can work better across levels, courses and streams than conventional format", says Aditya Malik, CEO and MD, Talentedge.

Aspects of E-learning

Although the foundation of education is still reading, writing and arithmetic, today's students need broader education. So, what can e-learning deliver?

1. **Live Instruction:** Certain curricula may require specialized instructors. By using live broadcasts, these instructors can remain in one location and provide instruction to many students in other locations. This type of specialization increases as students move into higher levels of education, for example, towards advanced degrees in medicine.
2. **Video Content Delivery:** Pre-recorded content such as lectures, documentaries and other video content may be delivered in a store and forward model so that the material can be viewed when needed.
3. **Student-to-student Interactions (Video Conferencing):** Students may learn just as much from each other as they do from teachers. Hence, communications technology can be used to connect students.
4. **Remote Test Administration:** In some countries, standardized tests are used to evaluate students on a level-playing field. These tests must be delivered securely and on-time to meet the testing schedules. In Indonesia, this is a daunting task simply because of geography and population size. Digital delivery could be the solution.
5. **Up-to-date Materials:** Basics seldom change. However, virtually all textbooks must be updated. Textbooks are expensive to purchase, maintain and deliver. Digital delivery solves this issue when coupled with e-readers.
6. **Self-learning:** Computer-based training or self-paced

learning is common in higher education and trade-oriented learning. Kiosks to support this may be located close to under-served areas where populations already work.

At the higher educational level, collaboration is vital to research. Post-graduate students in remote locations may be able to consult instructors at the university when needed. For example, in the medical field, tele-medicine can only be facilitated using broadband.

Literature Review

Currently, there is an increasing interest in data mining and educational systems and this makes educational data mining as a new growing research community. Many university courses and corporate trainings are held in electronic learning environment.

Higher education throughout the world is delivering this through universities, colleges and other recognised academic institutes. Till date, these educational institutions are placed in a highly competitive environment and are intending to get more advantages. These organisations need more knowledge for better assessment, evaluation, planning and decision-making to remain competitive in the educational field. Nowadays, the biggest challenges the educational institutions face, are the growth of educational data and the usage of this to improve the quality of decisions to bring quality education.

Providing quality education to students is the goal of higher education institutions. Discovery of knowledge for prediction about students' performance is required in order to achieve this high level of quality in higher education system. The data mining techniques are used to extract hidden knowledge among the educational dataset.

Data mining is a powerful technology with great potential that can be used for the extraction of hidden predictive information from large databases. It integrates a large number of techniques from a variety of areas including databases, statistics, machine learning, data visualisation, and others. This technology can discover the hidden patterns and associations from the educational data.

Data mining technology is widely used in educational field to retrieve useful information from students' data. The concealed samples that are discovered can be used to analyse and resolve the problem arising in the educational field.

Educational data mining (EDM) is a recent trend where data mining methods are experimented for the improvement of student performance in academics. The main objective of EDM is to improve teaching-learning process.

According to Bansode (2016), there are different kinds of educational environments which include offline education (traditional classroom), e-learning and learning management system (LMS) and intelligent tutoring system. In traditional classroom educational system, some of the attributes related with higher education students incorporate their behaviour, attitude and staff-student relationship. Prediction and analysis of these attributes helps to improve the teaching-learning process and to also improve the academic performance of higher education students.

Due to the increasing popularity of e-learning, personalisation has emerged as an important need (Marwah Alian, 'A Shortest Adaptive Learning Path in E-Learning Systems: Mathematical View', 2009). E-learning system is providing courses tailored to different students with different learning rates and knowledge degree.

Different behaviour, attitudes and aptitudes of individuals affect their learning, and these learning environments need to be adapted according to these individual differences, in order to maximize learning outcomes. This is known as adaptive web-based e-learning. The goal of adaptive e-learning is to deliver the right content, to the right person, at the proper time, in the most appropriate way, any time, any place, any path, any pace.

According to Shweta Pawar (2015), online learning is the current boom in market. Adaptive e-learning will serve as a perfect platform to improve the current scenario by suggesting courses adapted to results, behaviours, preferences, learners, etc. systematically.

Ahmad Kardan (2013) opines that personalized curriculum sequencing is an important issue to achieve learning goals, especially in e-learning systems. The main challenge of the traditional teaching system is to provide courses suitable to different learners with different knowledge background. Therefore, many researchers developed adaptive learning path systems in order to promote the effectiveness and performance of learning process. Furthermore, an optimal adaptive learning path can help the learners in reducing the cognitive overload and disorientation.

Bhasker (2010) observes that selection of appropriate learning contents and delivery of them to learners are challenging tasks of e-learning, because the learning content must be provided to an acceptable level of the learner's understanding. In the literature, there are many approaches for generating learning paths. But the drawback of existing approaches are that they are not fulfilling all the learner's context such as profile context, infrastructure context, preference and learning context.

Therefore, a learning scheme has to be devised, which includes all the contexts of a learner. This helps the learner to get the most suitable study material. Since there are only learning path generation algorithms available in the literature, there is a necessity to devise algorithms for generating learning schemes. A genetic algorithm-based adaptive learning scheme generation algorithm is described in this paper.

C. Romero's (2007) paper surveys the application of data mining to traditional educational systems, particular web-based courses, well-known learning content management systems, and adaptive and intelligent web-based educational systems. Each of these systems has different data source and objectives for knowledge discovering. After pre-processing the available data in each case, data mining techniques can be applied: statistics and visualization; clustering, classification and outlier detection; association rule mining and pattern mining; and text mining. The success of the plentiful work needs much more specialized work in order for educational data mining to become a mature area.

Bansode (2016) explains that there are different kinds of educational environments. The author argues that the main objective of educational data mining (EDM) is to improve teaching-learning process. In this paper, students' performance is predicted using the decision tree method. Using this result, students whose performance is poor, can be warned. The management can take necessary action to improve their performance by giving more attention, taking extra lectures etc. These measures not only improve a student's performance, but also reduce the number of failures and help in improving college results.

Kartina Sin (2015) explains recent applications of big data technologies in education and presents a review of literature available on educational data mining and learning analytics. In the current learning environment, users learn in online communities like discussion forums, online chats, instant messaging and in various learning management systems like Moodle.

Students' activities through learning management systems create large amount of data that can be utilized in developing the learning environment, helping the students in learning and improving the overall learning experience. In addition to the data available from student activities, data is also created by educational institutions which use applications to manage courses, classes and students. The amount of data made available in the above scenarios is so enormous that traditional processing techniques cannot be used to process them.

Due to the limitations of the conventional data processing applications, educational institutions have started exploring "Big Data" technologies to process the educational data. The most popular techniques used in EDM are regression, nearest neighbour, clustering and classification. Some of the major topics in EDM are behaviour detection, performance prediction, adaptive learning, skill estimation, student modelling, game based learning, Q matrix, attrition risk prediction etc.

El-Halees (2009) explains how EDM can be used to analyse students' learning behaviour. After pre-processing the data, first they apply data mining techniques (decision trees, neural networks, k-nearest neighbour, naive bayes, support vector machines and many others) to discover different kinds of knowledge such as association, classification, and clustering and outlier detection rules. Then this knowledge is used to better understand students' behaviour, to assist instructors, to improve teaching, to evaluate and improve e-learning systems, to improve curriculums and many other benefits.

Kunyanuth Kularbphettong (2012) aims to discover the knowledge (or identify the variable which influences the student motivation behaviour) for analysing student motivation behaviour on e-learning. Application of data mining techniques such as association rules and classification techniques can indicate the important variables that influence the student motivation behaviour on e-learning. These techniques can be useful to model the student behaviour outcomes and the result can be used for the improvement of e-learning courses.

Elikia (2014) explains that educational institutes are restricted not only for predicting the academic performance of the students by considering internal and external marks and grades etc. It is also possible to create prediction models for predicting future details like career options and possibility for a teenage student to get violent in future.

In this paper, data mining technique classification was used in educational databases, to suggest career options for the high school students and also to predict the potentially violent behaviour among the students by including extra parameters other than the academic details. Rapid Miner has been used as the data mining tool. Various classifiers like ID3 (Iterative Dichotomizer) and C4.5 algorithm were used to give career suggestions and to find the violent behaviour in a student. As a future work, in this paper, it was suggested that different techniques like neural networks, SVM, K-NN, Naive Bayes and genetic algorithm can be used to make predictions more accurate.

Expanding E-learning

With the number of internet users in India expected to reach 250 million, rivalling the US and second only to China, India's potential as a huge market for e-learning is enormous. A large number of new users are accessing the internet for the first time from their smartphones, which is an ideal, personalised and commerce-enabled platform for e-learning adoption.

Universities will see more students accessing their coursework from outside the traditional classroom. As per the Docebo Report issued in July 2014, the worldwide market for self-paced e-learning reached US$ 35.6 billion in 2011. The five-year CAGR is estimated to be 7.6 percent, so revenues should reach US$ 51.5 billion by 2016. While the aggregate growth rate is 7.6 percent, several world regions have higher growth rates. The highest rate is in Asia at 17.3 percent, followed by Eastern Europe (16.9 percent), Africa (15.2 percent) and Latin America (14.6 percent).

According to another report, India's online education market size is set to grow to US$ 40 billion by 2017 from the current US$ 20 billion. India has one of the largest education systems in the world with a network of more than 1 million schools and 18,000 higher education institutions. More than half of the country's 1.2 billion population falls in the target market for education and related services.

E-learning brings unique advantages, the prominent being the ability to provide personalised attention to all students. In a conventional set up, this is only possible when a highly skilled tutor offers one-to-one tutorials. However, considering that most institutions have a classroom-based set up, such attention becomes difficult. Another advantage is that people living in smaller towns and cities can get access to the best possible learning resources from across the world, at a very affordable price. This helps create a level-playing field.

The developing wave of adaptive learning will help students with various levels of intellectual capabilities to glean the best from the learning process at their own pace, without feeling left out.

Online tutoring will definitely pose a threat to conventional methods of teaching—while online learning can never look at completely replacing schools because schools offer much more than just academic knowledge inside their campuses. However, private tuition centres will have to take a second look at their business model and adopt digital learning aids to sharpen their offerings.

Broadband Advantage with a Business Opportunity

Satellite broadband, typically VSAT (very small aperture terminal), is ideally suited to bridge this gap. In the past, satellite connectivity was typically thought of as too expensive, too slow and not reliable. With the advent of high throughput satellites (HTS) and advances in radio technology, the cost and reliability of satellite connectivity has made it an attractive option. Satellite broadband offers distinct advantages such as competitive cost, multicast capability, universal coverage and low-cost simple installation.

Further, specialised equipment such as digital whiteboards, video conferencing systems, multimedia systems and even 3D learning experiences may be connected to take advantage of the broadband connectivity.

As e-learning tools become more advanced, so does their bandwidth requirement. Depending on which applications are in use, bandwidth requirements can vary from several hundred kbps all the way to multi-megabit connections.

In underdeveloped and developing countries, e-learning raises the level of education, literacy and economic development. This is especially true for countries where technical education is expensive, opportunities are limited and economic disparities exist.

Thanks to satellite technology, the costs have come down so significantly that every student—whether a grade school student or medical student doing a rotation in a remote area—can take full advantage of bandwidth provided by broadband satellite systems.

Conclusion

The rapid increase in internet connectivity has been an important catalyst for the growth of e-learning. A robust internet ecosystem, with a multitude of local and global players, will help online learning make further inroads. The story is not limited to educational institutions alone. Indian companies are adopting e-learning platforms as continuous employee learning has become a strategic necessity. We can expect greater development in this spectrum in coming years as the concept of Digital India is going to flourish in its full vision.

References

Ahmad, A. and M. Kardan (2013), "A New Personalised Learning Path Genenration Method: ACO-Map", *Indian Journal of Computational Intelligence and Systems Sciences*, 19-24.

Bansode, J. (2016), "Mining Educational Data to Predct Students' Academic Perfomance", *International Journal of Recent and Innovation Trends in Computing and Communication* , 1-5.

Bhasker, M. (2010), "Genetic Algorithm Based Adaptive Learning Scheme Generation for Context Aware E-Learning", *International Journal of Computer Science and Engineering*, 1271-1279.

Brijesh, Kumar and S.P. Baradwaj (2011), "Mining Educational Data to Analyse Students' Performance", *International Journal of Advanced Computer Science and Applications*, 63-69.

Romero, C.S. (2007), "Educational Data Mining: A Survey from 1995 to 2005", *Expert Systems with Applications,* 135-146.

Elakia, G.J. (2014), "Application of Data Mining in Educational Database for Predicting Behavioral Patterns of the Students", *International Journal of Computer Science and Information Techologies*, 4649-4652.

El-Halees, A. (2009), "Minimg Students Data to Analyse Learning Behaviour", Department of Computer Science, Islamic University of Gaza, Palestine, 1-4.

Elikia, G. (2014), "Application of Data Mining in Educational Database for Predicting Behavioral Patterns of the Students", *International Journal of Computer Science and Information Technologies*, 4649-4652.

Kartina Sin, L.M. (2015), "Application of Big Data in Education Data Mining and Learning Analytics: A Literature Review", *ICTACT Journal of Onsoft Computing,* 1035-1049.

Kunyanuth Kularbphettong, C. T. (2012), "Mining Educational Data to Analyse the Student Motivation Behavior", World Academy of Science,Engineering and Technology, *International Journal of Computer, Electrical, Automation, Control and Information Engeneering*, 1032-1036.

Latha Parthiban, S.S. (2013), "Ant Colony Optimization for Adaptive Learning", *Indian Journal of Computational Intelligence and Systems Sciences*, 19-24.

Manal Abdulla, R.M. (2015), "The Impact of Learning Styles on Learner's Performance in E-learning Environment", *International Journal of Advanced Computer Science and Applications*, 24-31.

Marwah Alian, R.J. (2009), "A Shortest Adaptive Learning Path in e-Learning Sytems: Mathematical View", *Journal of American Science*, 32-42.

N. Sivakumar, R. (2015), "Determining Optimized Learning Path for an e-Learning System Using Ant Colony Optimization Algorithm", *Intrenational Journal of Computer Science and Engineering Technology*, 61-66.

N. Sivakumar, R. (2015), "Improving Content Personalization through Ant Optimization in e-Learning", *Advances in Natural Applied Sciences*, 581-586.

Nor Bahiah Hj Ahmad, S.M. (2010), "Granular Mining of Student's Learning Behaviour in Learning Management System Using Rough Set Technique", *Computational Intellegence for Tech Enhanced Learning,* 99-124.

Shweta Pawar, S.S. (2015), "A Proposed System for Adaptive e-Learning Using Ant Colony Optimization", *IJSART*, 72-76.

Sengupta, S.S. (2011), "Construction of Learning Path Using Ant Colony Optimization from a Frequent Pattern Graph", *International Journal of Computer Science*, 314-321.

10

Impact of MGNREGA on Livelihood Security of Rural Poor

C. Vinodan and Rajeev M.M.

Introduction

The Mahatma Gandhi National Rural Employment Guarantee Act (MGNAREGA) is considered as a milestone in social policy, employment creation and step towards ensuring livelihood security in India. It was mandated in 2005 to implement an ambitious, demand-driven employment-creation programme to benefit the rural poor. Guaranteeing the right of rural households to 100 days of unskilled manual work, the programmes' size sets a worldwide precedent. It has achieved impressive results, but the Act continues to pose immense design and management challenges. In order to get a sense of the impact of the Mahatma Gandhi National Rural Employment Guarantee Scheme (NREGS) and its usefulness to the rural masses in the country, this study attempted to identify the number of households using or benefitting from these assets and the area of land that was impacted by the work created under the Mahatma Gandhi NREGS, depending on the nature and sustainability of assets created, local economic development and livelihood security.

The Act is also an attempt to provide a *legal guarantee of employment* to anyone in rural areas willing to do casual manual labour at a *statutory minimum wage*. What makes the Mahatma Gandhi NREGS distinct from any other public employment programme is that it is a *universal* and *enforceable* legal right concurrent with some of the provisions of Article 391 and Article 412 of the Directive Principles of State Policy in the Indian

Constitution that enshrines the ideals of the Right to Work.

Nevertheless to say that, the impact of MGNREGA focusing on employment security, income generation, and its governance and future perspectives were dealt in the study. It was found that MGNREGA covered all poor sections of the rural society irrespective of caste, gender or social orders. It was also observed that this project enhanced income as well as savings of rural households. Further, it was noticed that MGNREGA has created rural employment opportunities. Mahatma Gandhi NREGA is the first ever law internationally that guarantees wage employment at an unprecedented scale. The primary objective of the Act is augmenting wage employment and its auxiliary objective is strengthening natural resource management through works that address causes of chronic poverty like drought, deforestation and soil erosion and hence encourage sustainable development. The process outcomes include strengthening grassroots processes of democracy and infusing transparency and accountability in governance.

MGNREGA has been implemented in three phases across the country. In the first phase, it was launched in 200 'backward' districts during 2006 (i.e. districts with low agricultural wages and productivity and a large proportion of scheduled castes/tribes (Planning Commission, 2003). In the second phase in 2007-2008, an additional 130 districts were covered. The programme was extended to the remainder of the 295 districts in phase three during 2008-2009. As the 66th round of the NSS survey was conducted during 2009-2010, we exclude MGNREGA phase three districts from this analysis, as it was too early to assess the impact of the programme using 2009-2010 NSS survey data. Hence, in our analysis, we include districts from only phases one and two.

NREGA stands for 'National Rural Employment Guarantee Act' (2005) enacted on September 2005 and brought into force with effect from February 2006 in 200 most backward districts and covering all districts of the country within the next five years. The objective of the Act is 'enhancement of livelihood security of rural households by providing at least one hundred days of guaranteed wage employment in every financial year to every household whose adult members volunteer to do unskilled manual work'. Simply put, the primary objective of the Act is 'enhancement of livelihood security in rural areas by providing 100 days of unskilled manual work' with the auxiliary objective being: generating productive assets, protecting the environment, empowering rural women, reducing rural-urban migration, and fostering social equity (MICARVAAN, 2008).

MGNREGA's overall goal is to enhance livelihood security. Livelihood security is a long-term impact goal that requires detailed microeconomic data as well as numerous control variables to evaluate. For instance, in addition to MGNREGA, a host of other factors impact rural livelihoods, such as weather, macroeconomic trends, education, and social constraints, among others. As a quantitative measure, livelihood security is thus too broad and far-reaching to be used for the purpose of monitoring (CBPS, 2012). The purpose of implementing NREGA is to provide basic livelihood facilities to the rural masses. The village economy would improve only when the livelihood position of the village people improves. The improvement in livelihood security and local economy will have corresponding change in the local markets especially in local business and the consumption patterns of the rural people. The primary focus of the study is to understand and analyse the local economic development of rural areas through the implementation of MGNREGS.

Review of Literature

Rural livelihoods constitute the economic, social and cultural universe wherein rural families are bound to make their living. Although farming is still an important activity in rural areas, it is increasingly unable to provide sufficient means of survival. Employment growth in the farm sector being stagnant, there is an increasing trend towards casualization of labour. Wage employment, both as agriculture labour and labour in allied services, constitutes a significant means of livelihood in rural India. Rural labour, which constitutes a large section of unorganized workforce in India, includes landless and poor households which typically rely on the sale of their labour in farm and non-farm activities.

The rural workforce suffers due to excessive seasonality of employment, lack of wage employment opportunities and low wage rates. These poor rural households practice multiple livelihoods and even resort to temporary or permanent migration to increase their employment days and cope with the risks. Ellis (2000) gives particular emphasis to the widespread strategy of rural livelihood diversification, which rural households pursue in order to survive and to improve their standard of living. The diversification of livelihood strategies is a rapid process and shows no signs of abating (Gupta, 2009).

Well, if we look at the status of implementation of this programme in India, the Act was initially notified in 200 most backward districts in Phase I and at present in its third phase, it covers 619 districts (99 percent of the districts in the country). An overview of the performance of MGNREGA since its inception suggests that it does provide basic income assurance to a large number of beneficiaries. During the financial year 2011-2012 alone, nearly 5.5 crore households (close to 25 percent of all rural households in the country) were benefited. The average wage per person-day has gone up by 81 percent since the Scheme's inception, with state-level variations. Scheduled castes (SCs) and scheduled tribes (STs) have accounted for 51 percent of the total person-days generated and women for 47 percent, well above the mandatory 33 percent as required by the Act. Also, 143 lakh works have been taken up since the beginning of the programme, of which about 60 percent have been completed (www.nrega.nic.in, December 2012).

Mahatma Gandhi National Rural Employment Guarantee

Act (MGNREGA) implemented by the Ministry of Rural Development (MoRD), is the flagship programme of the Government that directly touches lives of the poor and promotes inclusive growth. The Act aims at enhancing livelihood security of households in rural areas of the country by providing at least one hundred days of guaranteed wage employment in a financial year to every household whose adult members volunteer to do unskilled manual work. Mahatma Gandhi NREGA is the first ever law internationally that guarantees wage employment at an unprecedented scale. The primary objective of the Act is augmenting wage employment and its auxiliary objective is strengthening natural resource management through works that address causes of chronic poverty like drought, deforestation and soil erosion and so encourage sustainable development. The process outcomes include strengthening grassroots processes of democracy and infusing transparency and accountability in governance.

Jha et al., (2009) found that landholding of a household is a negative predictor of employment provided under NREGS in Rajasthan, suggesting better targeting in Rajasthan. However, the relationship turns positive in Andhra Pradesh suggesting programme capture by households with larger landholdings. This difference, according to them, arises due to varied level of land inequality in the two states (more inequality in AP than in Rajasthan) and higher ratio of NREGS wage to agricultural wage rates. Other determining factors are remoteness of the villages and greater political interference in AP. They also found evidence of complimentarity in both the states, between public distribution and NREGS employment, suggesting real income transfer through food subsidies.

The scheme has improved the lives of the people and has brought stability and assured income to the families that were until recently desperately poor (Vidya Subramanian, 2009). A study conducted by the Institute of Applied Manpower Research covering a sample of 6,000 households across 20 states in the country (300 samples per state) has revealed that the low earning level of a number of beneficiaries declined and the number of households reporting marginally higher income has increased (K. Balchand, 2009). In certain places, especially during the lean season, NREGA had been the only source of income (Sudha Narayan, 2008).

The above literature clearly indicates that the work done under MGNREGS is significant in nature but proper documentation of the entire exercises including success stories is a crucial element in understanding the intervention process and outcome of the programme. The current project will satisfy the needs of a comprehensive documentation of the best practices carried out at various villages under the project. With a budget of about 2.3 percent of total central government spending, MGNREGA is by far the best endowed anti-poverty programme in India (Ministry of Rural Development, 2008). It has attracted a considerable amount of academic interest due to its size and multidimensional implications for rural India.

Another notable characteristic of this programme is the coordination and integration of the scheme with the local/regional economic development process. Under Wage Guarantee Act, large sums of public investments are made. Leveraging these investments towards sustainable livelihood requires inter-sectoral convergence. Since, under the Act, planning is decentralized and funds transferred are untied, works can be planned, structured and executed as per local specific requirements. MGNREGA thus becomes a significant entry point for convergence with other development programmes related to irrigation, roads, water supply, housing, electrification, land and water development, drought proofing, etc.

Mathur (2007) suggests that while the Ministry of Rural Development is the nodal ministry at the centre, every relevant department and agency must be involved. The machinery of the entire government must act in concert and conscious and systematic efforts be made to marshal its combined energy, expertise and resource—as has been done only once before, for the Green Revolution. Hence, there is a need for proper orientation of functionaries involved, to understand the comprehensiveness of the scheme and design suitable interventions securing people's livelihoods.

Objectives of the Study

The study was carried out with the followings objectives:

1. To understand and analyse the local economic development of rural areas through the implementation of MGNREGS.
2. To understand the financial changes made by the programme among the women stakeholders.
3. To assess the influence and impact of the programme in agriculture and irrigation activities in the rural areas.
4. To make aware on the social usefulness of the programme in the community.
5. To suggest remedial measures, if necessary, based on the findings of the study.

Materials and Methods

The gram panchayats are the primary sampling unit. Purposive sampling method was used for conducting the study. Twenty gram panchayats were selected in the Kollam district. While selecting the gram panchayats, the following criteria were observed. The samples of 20 gram panchayats were selected for the purpose of the study. This includes two best performing panchayats, one least performing panchayat, and one panchayat with the highest number of SC population and 15 other panchayats. The 15 panchayats include both coastal and inland panchayats. These panchayats were selected on a random basis. There shall be at least one gram panchayat in each block panchayat of the district. Two gram panchayats which made best performance in the district during the year 2011-12 in providing employment in terms of number of households, generating person days and employment provided per household were selected. Two gram panchayats with low performance in the district during the year 2011-12 in terms of providing employment in terms of number of households, generating person days and employment provided per household were also selected. Gram panchayat/s of the district with maximum SC population and gram panchayat/s of the district with maximum ST population were also considered.

Selection of gram panchayats was done in consultation with the district programme coordinator and joint programme coordinator of MGNREGS. The information gathering in each sampling unit was done through interview with a cross-section of all stakeholders of MGNREGS. The total number selected for interview per sampling unit was 50 and out of this minimum 20-30 numbers were invariably beneficiary householders of MGNERGS. One FGD was conducted in each sampling unit with recorded beneficiaries/job card holders and non-beneficiaries, indirect beneficiaries etc.

Results and Discussion

This section presents an analysis of the important livelihood components such as changes in the financial status of the stakeholders and patterns found in the selected villages. Engagement of agricultural jobs, level of income increment of the respondents, issues in the agriculture sector, negative impacts of MGNREGS on the development of agricultural sector, and opinion on social usefulness of MGNREGS programme are discussed in this section. A total of 11 blocks of the Kollam district were included in the study. 1,000 respondents constituted the sample which included both beneficiaries and non-beneficiaries. A majority of the respondents were from blocks such as Chavara and Anchal and the lowest numbers of respondents were from blocks Pathanapuram and Vettikkavila. The percentage of respondents belonging to the general category was 40.6 percent. OBCs constituted 30.5 percent.

Respondents from scheduled caste and scheduled tribe were 12.4 percent and 2.7 percent respectively. These figures indicate that the percentage of beneficiaries belonging to the general category was higher than other categories. This also implies that the scheme did not have any kind of discrimination among the social groups and even the general category did not feel anything wrong in the participation of the employment. Majority of the respondents (78.6 percent) reported their salary to be below ₹ 1,000. And the respondents above ₹ 5,000 was very low (just 2.1 percent only). Thus, through this sample, it is evident that ultimately the current scheme is focused on the overall development of the people who were very poor and they sought to have income-oriented activity to sustain their livelihood. This again underlined the fact that the Mahatma Gandhi NREGS in the district could bring a large part of the very poor people under the umbrella of economic empowerment. Tables 10.1 to 10.6 highlight the findings of the study.

Majority (87.7 percent) of the respondents agreed that involvement in the MGNREGS programme increased the level of consumption in the family (Table 10.1).

Table 10.1: Changes in the Financial Status

Item	Yes		No	
	Frequency	percent	Frequency	percent
Increased consumption level of the family	574	87.7	81	12.4
Obtaining tangible assets	220	33.6	435	66.4
Procuring financial assets	161	24.6	494	75.4
Helping settle the debts	227	34.7	428	65.3

Only 33.6 percent reported that participation in NREGS helped them buy tangible assets. Nearly one-fourth respondents (24.6 percent) reported that they were able to procure financial assets by associating with NREGS. It was seen that 34.7 percent respondents were able to clear off their debts due to their participation in NREGS.

Table 10.2 shows that 60.3 percent of the respondents had

engaged themselves in agricultural jobs as part of Mahatma Gandhi NREGS programme. Almost 40 percent of the respondents were not working in the field of agriculture as part of this programme. It is evident that most of the work carried out by the stakeholders was in agriculture and related work. Recent review of this scheme confirmed that the Government is likely to make it mandatory that 60 percent of work undertaken in a district under the job guarantee scheme should be linked to agriculture and allied activities. The Rural Development Ministry will incorporate the mandatory clause in Schedule-1 of the MGNREGA so that every state has to follow the norms designed to give a fillip to agriculture through labour-intensive work under the job scheme.

Table 10.2: Engagement in Agricultural Jobs

Response	Frequency (N)	Percent
Yes	395	60.3
No	260	39.7
Total	655	100.0

Table 10.3 gives an item-wise description of the agricultural jobs undertaken by the respondents as part of the MGNREGS programme. Major jobs undertaken included paddy cultivation (17.4 percent), coconut plantation (38.8 percent) and rubber plantation (32.6 percent). MGNREGA operational guidelines issued in February 2013 stipulate the formulation of a development plan to identify works that should be taken up in the district to generate employment and promote sustainable development.

In a similar way, the Agriculture Department usually prepares an annual plan for all districts to identify activities to be carried out in a financial year. To ensure that both plans are not implemented in a standalone manner, it is necessary that agriculture related works in annual plan and MGNREGA development plan complement each other. It would be ideal if both the plans should clearly indicate panchayat-wise action plan of agriculture related works to be undertaken through convergence with the approval of gram sabha. This can be facilitated in each district by collector/district programme coordinator for MGNREGA by closely coordinating with agriculture department authorities.

Table 10.3: Item-wise Engagement in Agricultural Jobs as Part of MGNREGS

Item	Response	Percent
Paddy cultivation	No	82.9
	Yes	17.4
Coconut plantation	No	61.2
	Yes	38.8
Rubber plantation	No	67.5
	Yes	32.6
Floriculture/fruit trees	No	99.5
	Yes	0.5
Vermi compost	No	100.0
Aquaculture	No	100.0
Fishing	No	99.8
	Yes	0.2
Sericulture	No	99.8
	Yes	0.2
Others	No	66.6
	Yes	33.4

Table 10.4 gives the details of the pre- and post-difference in the mean income of men and women after the implementation of the MGNREGS programme. The mean daily income of men was ₹ 452 before the initiation of the programme. After the programme it rose to ₹ 624.

There was a significant difference ($t = 32.9$, $p<0.001$) in the mean income before and after the implementation of the programme. Similarly, the mean daily income of women was ₹ 350 before the initiation of the programme. After the programme it rose to ₹ 517. There was a significant difference

($t = 37.8$, $p<0.001$) in the mean income before and after the implementation of the programme.

Table 10.4 Mean Income of Men and Women before and after the Implementation of MGNREGS

Item	Implementation Status	Mean Score (N=655)	't' value	'p' value
Daily income of men	After	624.35	32.991	<0.001
	Before	452.48		
Daily income of women	After	517.42	37.847	<0.001
	Before	350.75		

According to 44 percent respondents, there was a high level of increment in the income after the initiation of MGNREGS programme. Another 33.6 percent reported the increment level as 'medium'. During the FGDs with the respondents, it was pointed out that the Mahatma Gandhi NREGS programmes helped transfer income to poor unskilled rural households during slack agricultural seasons by providing them temporary employment in public work in rural areas, thereby enabling them to have smooth consumption spending.

The impact of Mahatma Gandhi NREGA on agriculture sector has been the subject of considerable debate among researchers and policy makers across the country. This study highlights the main issues in the agricultural sector. According to 29 percent respondents, barren land, unfit for agriculture is an issue. Less rain is an issue according to another 28.5 percent of the respondents.

Low productivity is an issue for 25.3 percent respondents and 36 percent reported poor irrigation facilities. A small section of the respondents reported (12 percent) that agricultural land getting transformed into barren land was the major issue. 29 percent highlighted that less rain and change climate was the pressing issue in the agricultural sector in the district. High production cost was an issue for 16 percent of the respondents.

The impact of Mahatma Gandhi NREGS on agriculture sector has been the subject of considerable debate among researchers and policymakers across the country. The survey finds that the Mahatma Gandhi NREGS has had a positive impact on labour force participation in the agricultural sector following its implementation.

This was highlighted in FGDs. The FGDs also suggested that the MGNREGS works related to the agriculture field should be assessed by the agricultural department and directions to appropriate agricultural work in accordance with the season should be provided by the agricultural department. It also suggested that temporary earning opportunities in periods of less agricultural activities in the rural areas should be given. In other words, the objective of the Act is to create durable assets and strengthen the livelihood resource base of the rural poor.

Table 10.5 shows that 58.2 percent considered the impact of MGNREGS as highly useful to resolve the agricultural sector issues in the Kollam district.

Table 10.5: Impact of MGNREGS in Solving Issues in the Agricultural Sector

Item	Opinion on the possibility	Frequency	Percent
Is MGNREGS useful to find solutions to the issues in agricultural sector?	Highly	381	58.2
	Average	191	29.2
	Low	73	11.1
	Nil	10	1.5
	Total	655	100

However, 29.2 percent opined that it could be useful at an 'average' level. Also, 11.1 percent said that MGNREGS could be useful only at a 'low' level.

MGNREGA has positive and negative impacts on agriculture and rural households as on one hand earning of the labour/small farmers from MGNREGA are being used in agriculture and household expenditure and on the other it is responsible for the increasing wage rate in agriculture.

The goals of MGNREGA are to provide social protection to the most vulnerable people living in rural India: livelihood security for the poor through creation of durable assets, water security, soil conservation and increased land productivity; drought-proofing and flood management in rural India; empowerment of the socially disadvantaged, especially women, scheduled castes and schedules tribes, through the processes of a rights-based legislation; strengthening of decentralized, participatory planning through convergence of various anti-poverty and livelihoods initiatives; deepening democracy at the grassroots by strengthening panchayati raj institutions; and effecting greater transparency and accountability in governance. These goals are thus indirectly related to agriculture.

From among the total respondents, 7.6 percent reported that Mahatma Gandhi NREGS had negatively impacted the development of agricultural sector in the district. A whopping majority (84 percent), however, did not feel that MGNREGS had not left any negative impact on the agricultural sector.

It is revealed in the FGDs, that in some of the panchayats, group farming was done by self-help groups, and was a successful model in the productive sector (Table 10.6).

The work was organized through the Kudumbashree project and the poor had a stake in the work right from the beginning. Works on individual land permitted under NREGA were irrigation facility, horticulture plantation and land development.

The works taken up under these facilities were irrigation facility, construction of dug well, farm pond, diggi, tanka, water hose and tank-cum-dug well, ground water recharge structure, construction/lining of water courses/irrigation channel and other works of irrigation facility popular in the area.

Table 10.6: Negative Impacts of MGNREGS on the Development of Agricultural Sector

Item	Opinion	Frequency	Percent
Is MGNREGA hampering the progress of Agricultural sector?	High	50	7.6
	Medium	18	2.7
	Low	37	5.6
	Not at all	550	84.0
	Total	655	100

According to the survey, 78.9 percent of the respondents noted that Mahatma Gandhi NREGS had led to an improvement in the irrigation facilities in the locality. The opinion of the respondents in terms of item-wise improvement of important irrigation facilities as per the data shows that a little less than half (43.9 percent) of the respondents reported improvement in the canal facilities, 27.2 percent reported improvement in the wells, almost half (49.4 percent) of them reported renovation of digging ponds and 30.2 percent reported construction of bunds for irrigation purpose.

The social relevance of a development programme like Mahatma Gandhi NREGS assumed greater significance in the Indian context. This study also assessed the social usefulness of the Mahatma Gandhi NREGS programme in the Kollam district. It revealed that almost all sections (98 percent) of the respondents underlined the social relevance of the Mahatma Gandhi NREGS and highlighted the need for sustainability of the programme. The FGDs and validation workshops also supported this argument.

As regards the opinion of the respondents in terms of item-wise improvement of important irrigation facilities, a little less than half (43.9 percent) of the respondents reported improvement in the canal facilities, 27.2 percent reported improvement in the wells, almost half (49.4 percent) of them reported renovation of digging ponds and 30.2 percent reported construction of bunds for irrigation purpose.

The findings concluded that the impact of NREGA on

local labour markets was significant in the district in many ways. The programme had increased rural labour participation rates by drawing into the workforce many who were not active workers in the past due to their family constraints and social inhibitions. Now, they consider Mahatma Gandhi NREGS as a governmental programme aimed at improving their living standards. The study also finds that the scheme has created labour shortages in the conventional rural labour market. A section of people who were already engaging in land development and other works in the rural labour market are seeking MGNREGS for work. The FGDs also validated these findings. It also shows significant improvements in wages in the local labour market.

Conclusions and Recommendations

Participation of registered trade union workers in agricultural works under the MGNREGS helps them to properly articulate their interest and grievances about the scheme and to further workers' perspective in the design of the programme. The MGNREGA works related to the agricultural field should be assessed by the agricultural department and directions to appropriate agricultural work in accordance with the season should be provided.

MGNREGA programmes were to transfer income to poor unskilled rural households during slack agricultural seasons by providing them temporary employment in public work in rural areas, thereby enabling them to have smooth consumption patterns. The amendment of the Mahatma Gandhi NREGA is needed to introduce small-scale income generation activities such as stitching, pickle and food processing and value added products. Since the Mahatma Gandhi NREGS has put more burdens on panchayats, sufficient number of employees should be appointed. There is need for more effective implementation and awareness programmes for stakeholders. Provisions should be made to provide basic amenities for housing, drinking water and toilets, etc. under Indira Awaas Yojana

(IAY), Accelerated Rural Water Supply Programme (ARWSP) and Total Sanitation Campaign (TSC).

Linking Mahatma Gandhi NREGS with these programmes will enhance the welfare and well-being of the vulnerable sections of the rural population. In sum, the above analysis makes it clear that the Mahatma Gandhi NREGS has become a stable and sustainable social and economic development scheme initiated for the welfare of the weaker and marginalised sections of the society. It is found that almost all workers of this scheme have benefited from the programme in various ways such as developing leadership qualities, improving social relationship, initiating savings and improving financial management.

References

Balchand. K. (2009), "NREGA Lifts up Standard of Living", *The Hindu*, September 6, p. 18.

Ellis, F. (2000), "Rural Livelihoods and Diversity in Developing Countries", Oxford: Oxford University Press.

Gupta, M.S. (2009), "Labour and Sustainable Development", New Delhi: Serial Publications.

Jha, R. et al. (2009), "Capture of Anti-Poverty Programs: An Analysis of the National Rural Employment Guarantee Program in India", *Journal of Asian Economics*.

Mathur, L. (2007), "Employment Guarantee: Progress So Far", *Economic and Political Weekly*, 29(52): 17-20.

MGNREGA (2009), Ministry of Rural Development, Government of India, MGNREGA Division.

MICARVAAN (2008), "The National Rural Employment Guarantee Scheme (NREGS) in West Bengal: A Study of Sustainable Livelihood Models".

Ministry of Rural Development (2012), "MGNREGA Sameeksha: An Anthology of Research Studies on the Mahatma Gandhi National Rural Employment Guarantee Act, 2005: 2006-2012", New Delhi: Government of India.

Planning Commission (2003), "Report of the Taskforce on Identification of District for Wage and Self-employment Programmes", New Delhi: Government of India.

Sarda, Prasad (2007), "MGNREGA: A New Hope from NDA

Government", New Delhi: JNU.

Subramanian, Vidya (2009), "Social and Political Dividend from NREGA", *The Hindu.*

Sudha, Narayanan (2008), "Employment Guarantee, Women's Work and Childcare", *Economic and Political Weekly*, September 10-14.

11

Associations in Democracies: Some Theoretical Issues in the Indian Context

Praveen Kumar

Introduction

Associationalism in liberal theory is taken to mean an expression of individual's collective power achieved through combining a person's capabilities to organise himself or herself with similar capabilities of others in order to achieve common objectives that may not be catered for by the routine functioning of the state. This is assumed to be happening in a space where state may have a limited or no role. Another aspect is linked to the very ethos of liberal philosophy. It would give primacy to individual over the community. The liberal idea, in its core, has always focused on centrality of individuals. The state while respecting this tradition would not impose a preferred way of life. The state would leave its citizens as free as possible to choose their own values and ends consistent with a similar liberty for others (Sandel, 1984: 1-3).

Individuals are rational beings to the extent that they are capable of making judgements in favour of what is 'good', as in the case of followers of J.S. Mill or 'right', as in the case of Kantian liberals. On this view, then, individual is prior to the community, and the individuals cannot be treated not as a means to some other end. In this light, the associational engagements may be of value to the extent that they serve as a means to an individual's end. This way, it is individual's needs, capabilities and achievements that matter if the role of associational engagements is to be of value in a democratic set up. Hence, the capacity of the associations to return values to its members may be conditioned by an individual member's resources. Here, the role of individual initiative and leadership capabilities become an imperative to be factored into while studying the associational form of engagements and their relationship with democratic polity.

Associational role in furtherance of individual or collective interests is unlikely to happen without the support of the state. This is due to the legitimacy aspect of the state and its power to accord legitimacy to associational activities on its sovereign territory. The state is also the sole arbiter, in the eventual analysis, of 'right and wrong' and 'good and bad'. Also, it is the responsibility of the state to regulate functioning of associations in general welfare and lay down the procedures as how the associations should function. Further, the state is also, legitimately, the sole provider and guarantor of security of a person's life, liberty, property and dignity and an ultimate controller of all the resources on its territory and offshore resources belonging to it. The state, still, is the only capable agency that can take political decisions to undertake re-distribution of goods and services and grant favour or award punishment to individuals and groups.

Aspects related to association democracy linkages have been significantly analysed by a large number of scholars. [1] However, following Archon Fung, associations can be seen in their six functional roles with respect to the democratic theory (Fung, 2003). According to Fung's classification, briefly stated, *first*, associations have intrinsic value. *Second*, citizens learn civic socialisation and get political education on associational platforms. [2] *Third*, associations, as organisation of people on a common platform for the promotion of or protection of particular interests, also mean collective strength that can offer resistance against unconstitutional actions of state authorities and are also bulwark against any other concentrated interests, which may infringe upon life, liberty and property of individual citizens. *Fourth*, associations help improve ways in which interests are represented to lawmakers and translated into law and policy. *Fifth*, associations facilitate public deliberation. *Finally*, associations are also seen in their role as alternative means of governance, what Hirst had called as "an alternative to top down bureaucracy in the competent provision of services" (Hirst, 1994: 6).

The most influential of the arguments, however, has come from Tocqueville and those who are influenced by him. Robert Putnam, the most notable among the latter, highlighted the importance of horizontal associations including professional groups, cultural groups, literary guilds, choral societies and service groups. Putnam argued that participation in such associations generates networks, norms of reciprocity and trust, which help social cooperation to take place in a better way. He also argued that higher density of such associations in a region is an indication of better institutional functioning, and hence democracy, in that area. Putnam, on the other hand, underlined that the hierarchical nature of vertical associations prevents higher level of participation from the members. Mutual cooperation among them may be absent and hence vertical associations are not suitable to enhance social cooperation. On Putnam's accounts, thus, vertical associations have limitations in contributing to the democratic governance (Putnam et al., 1993: 173).

Putnam thought that horizontal associations are important in democracy because individuals interacting with one another on associational platforms create 'social capital'. Social capital, according to him, is created out of "social networks and the associated norms of reciprocity", and "like physical and human capital, social capital creates value, both in individual and as collective", and this is also a form of 'capital', "because we can 'invest' in networking". He considers that "some forms of social capital are good for democracy and social health, others are (or threaten to be) destructive" (Putnam and Goss, 2002: 8-11). Putnam makes a distinction, among others, between the "bridging" versus "bonding" social capital which is significant (Putnam, 2000:

22). He identified bonding social capital as those which bring together people who are like one another in important aspects (ethnicity, race, gender, social class) while the bridging social capital refers to social networks that bring together people who are unlike one another (people with diverse backgrounds). He added that the external effects of the bridging social capital are likely to be positive.

This understanding on association-democracy linkages needs qualification when it comes to explaining the process of democratisation and political liberalisation in the case of India. In Western liberal theory, a person's identity is that of an 'unencumbered self'. In contrast, the Indian society treats individuals as situated selves in terms of their identities 'being' always underpinned by some form of community membership.

Need for a Perspective in the Indian Context

Indian democracy has provided an extremely valuable site for the study of the associational functioning and its linkages to democracy. The evolution of democratic politics and representative government has its roots in various kinds of associational functioning since the period of national movement. The associational activities during the 19th century in India were centred on reformist ideas of individual leaders, who founded various kinds of societies or associations to fight against the social evils. Later associations aimed to counter British government's discriminatory policies against Indians in the administration. Associational activities also culminated in political activities; formation of Indian National Conference in 1883, for instance. Hardgrave has commented that it is out of associational politics that the Congress emerged first as an 'association for the political regeneration of India',(Hardgrave, Jr., 1970: 22-25) and later as a political party that steered the national movement successfully to usher India into a republican and representative form of political system. In the context of Indian democracy, other forms of group activities, caste, community or cultural groups too can be considered to have "incipient capability" to aggregate individual demands with others.

Post-Independence experiences with Indian democracy show that in spite of all the glaring contradictions, democracy has stood the test of time in India. Democracy has not only endured, "it has developed into a vibrant system" (Hasan, 2010: 241). However, the conditions under which democracy has taken roots in India are not similar to those of France or America, the cases, which were subjects of Tocqueville's comparative study. What Tocqueville understood in terms of 'transition to democracy' may be more applicable in the sense that this is a process that involves "the much slower, problematical, historical transition from pre-modern forms of society to a society shaped either wholly or in part by a democratic social imaginary" (Kaviraj, 2012: 20).

Also, due to the hierarchical caste structure and diversity of social conditions in India, democracy cannot be seen as providential design, but "rather as willed modifications by human action". In India, the role of political elites was crucial to produce a new social order based on political equality. This change was brought about "without a general collapse of faith and the moral order—which was Tocqueville's predominant anxiety" (Ibid: 24-28). Further, Tocquevillean experience of American democracy also suggests that democracy favoured transition from agrarian form of production to that of industrial form of production and transformation of the agrarian population into an industrial working class. However, the Indian society in the early decades of Independence was still "marked by persistence of various pre-capitalist forms of agricultural and craft production and the resilience of older ties of bondage between patron and client". By this description, the Tocquevillean views of American democracy cannot be applied in the Indian context (Chaterjee, 2012: 283).

Democratic traditions under Indian conditions were partly influenced by the colonial legacy. Features of the Indian Constitution, like representative government, legal equality and civil rights, and judiciary that functions independent of the executive, among others, are some of the manifestations (Sarkar, 2001: 23). Kohli, in this context, contends that Indian conditions defy theories based on various parameters such as the level of industrialisation, economic development, size of the middle class and civic culture, which have been applied to explain the strength of democracy in the Western context. The Indian state has achieved a reasonable level of democratisation, "amidst a low-income economy, widespread poverty and illiteracy, and immense ethnic diversity" (Kohli, 2001: 1) in terms of functioning of state institutions since it won Independence in 1947. The state institutions are also designed to address fairness issue to the weaker sections. The Indian society despite being multi-ethnic, multi-lingual and multicultural is characterised by inclusive government, cultural autonomy and safeguards for the weaker sections/minorities (Lijphart, 2008: 42-45).

The correlation between associational living and democracy has to factor in other values that are attached to the Indian conditions. One, associational life in India does not take place in a formally organised manner alone. Second, the associations that are active in various fields may not be helpful in contributing to democratic politics. If activities of non-profit organisations are taken as an indicator, then, as observed by Pradeep Chhibber and Rahul Verma, "India has approximately 3.3 million non-profit organisations...Despite these large numbers, civil society organisations in India have failed to provide citizens the resources they need to meaningfully engage in democratic politics" (Chhibber and Verma, 2013).

In the background of growing literacy and socio-economic equalities in India, the process of democratisation also means, among other things, awareness among the citizens for their political rights and social status. Further, successful completion of term by the elected governments and handing over power through electoral means has also been considered a sign of successful functioning of India's democracy, as most of the nascent democratic regimes in Asia and Africa have fallen prey to military dictatorships on various occasions in the past. In addition, the democratic state also must ensure a regime that is free of incidents of political violence. The state is expected to remain vigilant in cases where violence is likely to occur. Successful prevention of such happenings by the state is considered as examples that the state has positively contributed to the functioning of India's democracy.

India has also emerged as one of the fastest growing economies, only next to China. However, the social progress in India has not taken place at the same scale when compared with other growing economies like Brazil or China on parameters like per capita income, health care and sanitation facilities, and literacy, among others (Dreze and Sen, 2014: 66). Despite that, India's democracy can be characterised as politically vibrant. Ascriptive groups are seen in functional role in Indian politics. The caste system, among them, provides for hierarchical organisation of the groups in the system, even as on Putnam's accounts, this would fall within the purview of vertical organisations. Functioning of democracy in India, thus, has its context, which during its evolution has aimed to achieve inclusion as regards participation in the decision-making process and stakes in public resources.

In the Indian context, liberal individualism was always seen as a contested concept. National identities were always seen being constructed through national communities—caste, religious, ethnic groups. The language of politics was 'non-individualistic'. Community was defined in various ways. There always has remained a tension between the community as the bearer of rights and the individual. This was later manifested in the Indian Constitution; positive discrimination offered to the sections of the weaker caste groups is an instance.

The role of caste/communities in terms of group aggregation and interest articulation was considered important. Political parties, too, have mobilised support by effectively using these identities. Kaviraj has observed that "Although no single party derived benefit, all of them conspired to legitimise the idea that electoral politics must be carried out, realistically, in the language of community demands and grievances, rather than individual rights" (Kaviraj, 2012: 35). On this account, 'richness' of the present day democratic system and role of associationalism in India are not quite comparable to those of other societies in the West, where social formations do not quite follow hierarchical structures.

Caste associations in Indian politics have acted as institutions, which enable members to pursue social mobility, political power, and economic advantage. These could be understood as 'paracommunities' and appear similar, in many ways, to what Susanne and Llyod Rudolph state as "voluntary associations or interest groups familiar to European and American politics" (Rudolph and Rudoph, 1968: 29). [3] Their existence and functioning have contributed to the mobilisation process and political awareness of the members. Caste groups, especially in their functional role and seen vis-à-vis other caste groups have in themselves certain degree of 'social capital' and 'norms of reciprocity' present, rather in an ascriptive form. This form of connectedness is directed inward and the groups are cohesive and largely closed in nature. To borrow Putnam's distinction, these groups, at best, offered the conditions of 'bonding social capital' and not 'bridging social capital'. However, even under these conditions, democracy in the Indian context has evolved more in terms of participation and inclusion (Vora and Palshikar, 2004: 18).

Caste associations, especially those of the backward castes have played a role that undermined the hold of traditional power hierarchy in the Indian society. Susanne and Llyod Rudolph consider that associational activities in India, if seen in the Western sense, appear "confined to the urban-educated, who are more or less attuned to the modern political culture" (Rudolph and Rudolph, 2008: 4). However, in the Indian case, caste becomes a category of intra-group solidarity on various associational platforms. The tendency of attaching significance to caste and community over associational matters is prevalent among the urban educated middle class also. Further, this has been observed that caste associations in many cases were started as voluntary organisations of people of the same general caste. These associations were meant to setting and enforcing caste rules, frequently as part of *sanskritisation* process. The caste associations grew in resources and also became the target of political parties who woo them for electoral support (Rosen, 1966: 76).

Rajni Kothari also considers 'caste in a federal form', perhaps as an alternative to the "interest organisations of the Western form" (Kothari, 1970: 87). Highlighting this aspect of associational engagement, Kothari has viewed caste in their associational form as abridging the hierarchical rigidities and adapting the indigenous social structure to the exigencies of democratic political institutions.

If the level of associational activities is taken as an indicator, Pradeep Chhibber in a study has shown that only 13 percent of all Indians belonged to an association in 1991. This figure then was the lowest of the twenty five democracies (Chhiber, 1999: 17). Later, Chhibber writing with Verma quotes National Election Study of 2009 to state that "only about one in five Indian citizens belong to a formal association" (Chhiber and Verma, 2013). There may not be the same level or kind of connection between associational activities and democracy as has been emphasised in the literature of Tocqueville or Putnam or those that follow them. Associations could, at occasions, facilitate interactions and better understanding as regards rights and freedoms of the individual members and in this sense being instrumental in promoting the cause of democracy. However, this is not a one-way process, in a sense that the democratic environment, too, is a necessary condition.

The Indian system does not reflect characteristics that would establish a linear relationship between the presence of associations and richness of democracy. Meaning, we cannot assume that since India is a democracy and hence would have rich associational life or vice versa. In addition, influence of modernity and liberal democratic ideas was a factor behind mobilisation of the caste groups at various levels. In the Indian context, there has been influence of socio-political processes on the social identities—internally and externally. The Indian political process, thus offers an example where caste and community, in their collective form, could negotiate political resources for the members. To come together on other forms of associational engagement, the individuals needed to choose a new form of bonding (that would give rise to bridging social capital) over and above the ascriptive one. Given this background, associations in the Indian context may not respond the characteristics that we find in the literature surrounding the social capital debate, as Nadia Molenaers has also observed in her study of two Nicaraguan villages that "The link with trust, reciprocity, and horizontal cooperation is not to be generalised" (Molenaers, 2005: 164-165).

Measuring Democracy through Social Capital

Anirudh Krishna examined Putnam's claim and added that "capable agency is necessary in addition to high social capital for robust democracy". His idea was to see whether social capital provides both glue and gear or whether gear needs to be provided separately by a political party or some other type of agency. He has raised questions related to political participation in general and social capital more specifically in the context of rural India, in the States of Rajasthan and Madhya Pradesh. Following measurement of 'social capital' in 69 village communities, he has concluded that "social capital provides only the glue that makes collective action possible". To gear collective action towards participation in democracy, capable agency is separately required. Among other factors, groups and individual actors were significantly associated with higher participation rates (Krishna, 2002: 456).

Blomkvist and Swain have observed that in the Indian State of Orissa, in the post-Independence period, the coastal region has been politically and economically more powerful than the inland region. According to them, the inland part of Orissa does not protest as often as their coastal counterparts, and if protests occur, they are not sustained. They conclude that this is due to failure of different groups coming together. Strong communal 'bonding social capital' ties prevent the coming together for a common cause. It not only restricts associational life, but also curbs popular mobilisation (Blomkvist and Swain, 2001: 641).

In his study of Talajanga village in Orissa's Puri district, Bishnu Mohapatra examined social capital by exploring the nature of connectedness among people in a context of inequality, segmentation and institutional decline. He has concluded that trust/social capital alone cannot help people to get things from public/state institutions. Internal coordination worked fine but not the external ones (Mohapatra, 2001: 665-672). Likewise, in her study of Teri and Garhwal districts of erstwhile Uttar Pradesh (now Uttarakhand), Nirja Gopal Jayal has found out that "social capital cannot be understood outside of its particular cultural, ideological and institutional contexts" (Jayal, 2001: 655-664).

In her study, in the context of politics of identity in Uttar Pradesh, of six gram panchayats and their samitis (committee) in selected blocks of the two districts—Meerut and Azamgarh, Sudha Pai has examined if democratic decentralisation introduced by the 73rd amendment of the Indian Constitution has led to a greater participation by and successful implementation of government funded programmes for the lower castes. The study looks into role of panchayats in resolution of conflicts that takes place among social groups competing for the benefits of development, what she calls, "based upon the creation of common norms, values, trust and collective action or are they an arena of conflict and contestation over scarce resources, social status and political power". Her findings show that in India, "segmentation arising out of caste/class divisions emerges as a significant contextual variable determining the development of trust, social capital, between groups and democratic functioning of the institutions" (Pai, 2001: 652).

She further explained that faster political mobilisation through socio-cultural movements in civil societies and political parties thrown up by democratisation has united disadvantaged groups creating larger identities of *dalits* and most backward castes (MBCs) that have challenged upper/middle caste dominance. Also, capitalist development and state funded welfare programmes have sharpened competition and conflict between *dalits* and *MBCs* and sub-castes within them for control over economic resources, social status and political domination.

Pai's study is an instance, where tension and conflicts at the local level are due to the competition for the public resources. The argument could be extended to suggest that villages being a small community and the level of informal interactions being quite high, this should produce certain level of trust among the dwellers. However, how public resources are managed at the local level becomes an important factor in the whole process.

Thus, even as certain degree of trust is assumed within the village *panchayats*, by virtue of the fact that villages being small communities and dwellers being mostly familiar with one-another, when it comes to staking a claim for the public resources, it is not the 'collective action' but 'collective competition' that guides the action of the local communities.

Social Capital and Inter-community Peace

Richness of democracy in the Indian context would also mean a process, which offers an environment that is free from or at least can restrain political violence, and create an environment of communal harmony. However, Indian state has not been free from occurrences of such violent incidents. Association-democracy linkages have been applied to explain that the regions in India, which have denser network of cross-community associations, are less prone to communal violence. By extension of the argument, it would be a positive contribution to democracy. The areas where networks of civic engagement, such as integrated business organizations, trade unions, political parties, and professional groups cross communal lines, violence appears controllable and the possibility for confrontations are less likely. Communally integrated associations could serve as an agent of peace. They have a restraining effect on those 'politicians' who would polarize Hindus and Muslims and "it is the environment of a peaceful city that makes the police and administration perform its law and order functions better" (Varshney, 2002: 289).

Further, there could be areas/localities, considered as potentially violent and they lack what can be termed as inter-community 'trust' or 'bonding'. In the conditions of the latter, occasions of provocations in the form of a trigger could lead to violence. The trigger could be in the form of an attack on a train, the rumour of a rape, defeat of ethnic political parties in elections and desecration of a mosque or a temple.

According to this theory, the cities in general may not be free from being influenced by such triggers, but presence of inter-community networks capable of facilitating inter-community dialogue should manage or extinguish those triggers. If civic engagement is only intra-ethnic, not inter-ethnic, small or unconfirmed rumours, like Hindu boys going out with Muslim girls, or vice-versa or pigs thrown into a mosque or killing of cows can lead to a high level of violence. Occasions of violence are also conditions when bonding or trust gets weakened between the communities, even as multi-ethnic society with strong interconnections across ethnic boundaries may manage turbulence. Civic networks, in the long-run, could also be politically constructed. However, where the organisations were integrated between the communities, violence is likely to be managed in favour of peace.

Regions, towns and villages in India have managed to remain

peaceful amidst ethnic or communal diversity. However, some regions/cities have also experienced enduring patterns of violence. There is a spatial pattern as well. Varshney has noted that the communal violence level among the villages in India is 'abysmally low', in comparison to the urban India. Within urban India, too, as Varshney finds, Hindu-Muslim riots are locally concentrated. Thus, cities could be identified, which are potentially prone to communal violence. State and national politics provide the context. Violence could very well be a local phenomenon. However, the pre-existing local networks of civic engagement between the two communities stand out as an important cause, which does not allow the tensions to deteriorate into rioting and violence.

The informal groupings, also mentioned above, should allow people to come together as temporary organisations during tensions. They would be short-term, but significant. Their membership, if cutting across communities, act as watchdog against untoward incidents or undesired rumours. They prove to be important during tension. They also act as 'responsible informer' for the local administration. Their role as dialogue facilitator between the communities during unrest is extremely important. Such organisations do not grow in cities where everyday interaction does not cross religious lines. In addition, vibrant organisations which serve the economic, cultural, social, and political needs of the two communities, the support for communal peace tends to be strong and is also more solidly expressed.

The larger political process taking place in the society is central to the functioning of the Indian democracy. This is true even for the places where the civic associations have strong presence across communities and smooth functioning of democracy is attributed to the latter. 'Communal conflict' involving Hindus and Muslims is considered an urban and not a rural phenomenon. On the basis of an original data set assembled from *The Times of India* reports from 1950 to 1995, Varshney has identified eight cities, Bombay (now Mumbai),

Ahmedabad, Hyderabad, Meerut, Aligarh, Baroda (now Vadodara), Delhi and Calcutta (now Kolkata) as being 'most riot prone'. Varshney has drawn paired comparisons, of Ahmedabad and Surat, Hyderabad and Lucknow, Aligarh and Calicut (now Kozhikode) to show the importance of the existence or absence of the kind of civic life that brings the members of the two religious communities together.

Varshney appears to be arguing that not 'social capital', but the extent to which various existing organisations, which bring people of different communities together and help to appreciate shared interests or identities matter in the violence free communal life and richness of democracy. In Kozhikode, the principal axis of social conflict has been based along caste/class identities. Both Hindus and Muslims have come together to serve their common interests. In Lucknow, the organisation of the *chikan* (embroidered textiles) industry has brought an element of mutual dependence between the Hindu businessmen and the masses of Muslim workers. The situation is such as "if communal riots were to break out, the local economy would collapse" (Varshney, 2002: 214).

Varshnney's arguments suggest that formal or informal associations which have common membership among the communities facilitate inter-community communication on issues of common concern. This helps in creating and strengthening of bonds between the communities, which fosters communal harmony, and by extension of this argument, this is a contribution to the robustness of democracy. However, issues such as social conflicts need to factor in reasons other than lack of 'bridging form of social capital' behind persistence of communal clashes in India. Violence occurs under conditions, which themselves are not inherently ethnic/communal in nature. Further, they could at best be ambiguous in character. Their "transformation into caste or communal incidents depends upon the attitudes towards them taken by local politicians and local representatives of state authority, and their ultimate elevation into grand communal confrontations depends upon their further reinterpretation by press and extra-local politicians and authorities".

Associational life in the Indian context and its role vis-à-vis democracy is not independent of the prevailing political environment. Associations, in their functional role, too bear the influence of larger political activity. Role of associations in acting as a 'bridge architect' between the communities through individual membership would facilitate inter-community dialogue to the extent that it has the support of the membership. This, on occasions, could have an important role in conflict-prevention. Conditions when community conflicts take place or civic order breaks down become occasions to test the hypothesis if closely knit networks are really contingent for the functioning of democracy. What are the other factors that could be identified behind rise of community conflicts? Are they case specific? Or, is a broader generalisation possible? Can associations be seen in their negative role? Do associations in their negative role support the argument that democracies could be better off without them?

In times of ethnic tensions, how rich associational life or to use Varshney's term, the civic engagement could potentially build bridges between the communities, need to be seen again as a part of the whole process. If civic engagement is crucial to 'communal peace', then this has to be pre-given for the communal peace. Varshney notes that possibilities of occurrences of inter-community conflict would be high if communities are organised only on intra-communal or intra-ethnic lines. The internal characteristics of the group would again be an added factor, like how the groups are organised and democratised within. If democracy is a valued concept and the overall prevailing environment is democratic, the occurrences of conflicts would, possibly, not be dependent only so much on the interconnections across the communities, say if the inter-communal engagement is either very weak or non-existent.

The conditions are not independent of local socio-political context. There are important considerations with respect to role of informal groupings and inter-community networks, like individual initiatives, prevailing environment, trust *not* because of the networks and role of state and its institutional set up at the local level. In addition, the discourse has to factor in diversity, ascriptive identity and group action under the influence of these two. An understanding of the association-democracy correlation would have to factor in these aspects, in addition to the role of 'social capital'.

Evaluating Associational Engagement in Indian Democracy

What can be understood in the light of the discussions above is that the influence of associational activities has been discussed and analysed variously to explain the condition of democracy with reference to functioning of public institutions and prevailing socio-political environment, both. In most of these discussions, the role of 'social capital' has been highlighted to see the resultant outcomes of the functioning of public institutions or prevailing norms of civic or political virtues as regards the public life in Indian society. Studies that bring out limitations of the 'social capital' theory in explaining the existing democratic standards in India were also discussed. These studies have also suggested that parameters other than social capital may be required to better explain the status of democratic institutions. It has been found out that the associational activities and resultant social capital need to be understood and explained with the help of local socio-political dynamics that includes role of caste and community, bonding that exists prior to and apart from associational activities, role of individual members and leaders on associational platforms and the larger political system.

There are various ways in which associations could be useful in strengthening democratic norms. The associational form of engagement in India can at best be characterised as what Charles Taylor has said, 'civil society in the minimal sense'. There are free associations, which are "not under the tutelage of state power", but the civil society functions "through associations and their integration with the state" (Taylor, 1995: 89-90).

Associational life under Indian conditions appears to be different in its form and role from what generally is the prevailing understanding, which attempts to characterise democracy as strong if associational engagement, particularly the cross-boundary engagement is high. Community or caste-based associations are likely to be inward looking in character. They cement the 'bonding social capital'. The associations, which may have 'diverse' membership, also show signs of more 'bonding social capital', albeit in pockets, than the 'bridging social capital'. The membership may cut cross caste/community, but individuals are closer to their caste/community members more in comparison to the others while active within the association and this also leads to emergence of distinct groups within the associations. Thus, consolidation along caste/community lines becomes an obvious feature of the Indian associational life.

On the members' activities in such associations, it would be found that the 'generalised reciprocity' that Putnam has attached great significance to, is not a general attribute of associational living (Putnam, 2000: 134). Putnam contended that on associational platforms, members tend to help each other with an understanding that I do something for you so that you (or someone else) shall return this favour when I need it (which he called 'generalised reciprocity'). This form of generalised reciprocity has two aspects as regards associational life in India. One, informal inter-communal engagement that Varshney has called 'quotidian' is more prominently displayed and the kind of 'generalised reciprocity' that Putnam has discussed takes place much more in this sphere of engagement than on the associational platform. Secondly, on associational platforms, this depends on individual members' ability/resources to do or return a favour, in addition to his or her willingness.

The whole idea of inculcation of various kinds of civic virtues in individual members that would make democracy robust rests on an understanding that these civic virtues are generated through participation in associational activities. The kind of civic virtue leading to robust democracy that the Western literature on the discourse has emphasised is not generated out of associational activities in the Indian case. There are forms of associational activities that function the other way round, if seen from this point of view.

Partha Chaterjee's observations on street vendors and private transport operators in India are significant in this regard (Chaterjee, 2010: 9-10). He says that street vendors who occupy street place are seen violating municipal laws. They use municipal services water and electricity, but pay no taxes. For their business under such environment they usually organise themselves into associations to deal with state institutions like the municipal authorities, the police, banks and corporate firms. These associations are large in terms of the number of members and the geographical spread, and the volume of trade they encompass could be considerably high. The vendors operate within a "public and anonymous market situation and are subject to standard conditions of profitability of their business". The associations also restrict the number of vendors in a given area to ensure that the vendors engaged in the business are able to meet their livelihood needs in a given area. However, such associations may allow new members if the business is doing well.

Similar observations were made by Chaterjee in the case of associations which are active in the field of transport sector. Thus, these associations are working towards some objectives and serving the interests of their members, but have evolved their own methodology to deal with public institutions or similar interests operating outside their activity area. These associations are examples of the kind which are meant to work against the established norms of 'civic virtue', like respect for the laws, paying timely taxes, opposing corruption in public places and services and respecting similar rights of others.

In India, participation level of individual members in

associational activities is mostly low. Free-riders' syndrome could be high as the understanding may prevail that what is the need to make endeavours on issues which is likely to affect everyone equally. Further, if everyone is an affected party, then someone would do something to address the issue and to which they would be natural and equal beneficiary. Moreover, the associations have leaders and office-bearers. It is the leadership that should accomplish the tasks for the members.

As a result, the leaders in these associations, owing to apathy of the general members, steer the functioning of the associations in a manner that they consider is fit and eventually what suits them. The feeling that 'checks and balances' are generally absent, may make the leaders gradually indifferent to the controls that should come from the scrutiny of their actions by the general members. Resources of the association may be utililised as per their wishes. This eventually would influence the objectives of the associations. Participation is also subject to leaders' efforts in mobilising the members in general, and this way the associational activities can also be characterised as a form of 'guided collective action'.

Thus, the kind of relation that has been emphasised in the context of other societies that associations encourage participation and participation inculcates civic virtues in individual members, which eventually contributes in the strength of democracy is not quite clear in the Indian context.

Associations are certainly good platforms where people interact and intermingle with fellow citizens, but this happens within the constraints that we have seen in the above paragraphs. Participation may also depend on socio-economic factors and resources available to the individual members, which includes material, time and civic skills (Verba et al., 1995: 271-294). Individuals with better economic and educational background may occupy important positions and active in associations' affairs more than the general membership.

Associational functioning comes with the support of the

larger political community. State agencies are actively involved in lending support to the activities of the civil society groups. As regards Varshney's thesis that high level of inter-communal engagement puts checks on communal conflicts, it needs underlining that other factors like vested interests, role of criminal gangs and political rivalries are important aspects to understand in such situations. [4]

In addition, individual interests exploit vulnerable occasions at the high points in the declining inter-community trust. Business interest is yet another factor, which shape individual behaviour in exploiting community identity for personal gains. This is linked to business competition between the members of different communities. Members from different communities interact with each other on the basis of personal initiative and acquaintance and interactions are generally routine in nature, thus, the quotidian form of engagement becomes prominent. Associational activities are characterised more by 'bonding social capital' than the 'bridging social capital'. Thus, communication may occur between the community members on a routine basis, but this may not foster the kind of civic ties that the association-democracy theory would expect them to generate.

Associations may be platforms that foster debate among the members and setting up the agenda for deliberative politics. However, only a small group could be found to be active in the association. The scope of debate on associational platforms may be limited as office bearers prima facie may reach some understanding beforehand on the issues that should be brought before the general members. In addition, lower level of participation from the members may allow the office bearers and leaders to set the agenda and steer the debate in the direction of their choice. Thus, informal engagement between the members, again, appears to be an important aspect of an associational life.

In addition, the affairs within the association could be 'vote-centric' and the members are not in the habit of exercising the choice of deliberative politics that the associational platforms would offer. Associations offer opportunities where equal and open communication process may happen and in which participants can discuss the issues of their concern and make others understand their point of view, but this choice would not be exercised. People may discuss issues of their concern at places where they routinely gather, like tea stalls or paan shops, for instance.

Overall, the associational platforms may not be utilised to their potential. Individual engagement in his or her day to day issues would take more priorities than the role as members of different associations. Becoming part of associations would result in taking interest in the day to day affairs of the association due to other priorities in life, which includes earnings, health care, providing basic amenities to their families and better education for the children, among others.

Conclusion

As the discussions above show, representation and accommodation of diverse interests is a key for a smooth and peaceful functioning of the public life. The associational form of engagement need not be seen through the prism of established theories that have been discussed in the previous paragraphs. The context could be particular to Indian conditions and the evolution of associational politics can be situated in this context. This could be seen as a process and not an evaluation of associational engagement strictly in terms of their successes or failures in contributing to the robustness of democracy. Further, India's democracy itself is still taking its shape as a result of various socio-cultural and economic-political processes at work. The Indian scenario rightly provides space for dissent and differences. If democracy is seen as nurturing and cherishing of local and particular interests, in addition to representative institutions for governance, the Indian democratic system truly provides an environment where associational forms of engagement of various shapes are taking place in the public arena.

Notes

1. Warren, Mark E. (2001), "Democracy and Association", New Jersey: Princeton University Press; Cohen, Joshua and Joel Rogers (1992), "Associations in Democratic Governance", in 'Politics and Society', 20(4); Carter, April and Jeoffery Stokes (2002) (eds.), 'Democratic Theory Today', Cambridge: Polity Press; Gutman, Amy (1998), "Freedom of Association: An Introductory Essay", Gutman, Amy (ed.), "Freedom of Association", Princeton: Princeton University Press.
2. As democracies provide spaces for variety of associations and each association is capable of inculcating similar values in their members, different groups can negotiate differences among themselves and this is helpful in, what Iris Marion Young has called "furthering the idea of democracy". Associations, thus, "instil in their members habits of cooperation, solidarity, and public spiritedness". They foster adherence to 'generalized reciprocity' in their members, which Robert Putnam has explained as, "I'll do for you now, without expecting anything immediately in return and perhaps even without even knowing you, confident that down the road you or someone else will return the favour". Young, Iris Marion (1999), "Polity and Group Difference: A Critique of the Ideal of Universal Citizenship", *Ethics*, Vol. 99, 250-274.
3. Susanne and Lloyd Rudolph have noted that "horizontal mobilisation illustrates most clearly how the cultural and structural transformation of a traditional institution contributes to political modernisation and democracy, including political participation and representation". See Rudolph, Susanne Hoeber and Lloyd I. Rudolph (1968), "The Modernity of Tradition: Political Development in India", Chicago: University of Chicago Press, 29.
4. Electoral interests of the political leaders from Hindu and Muslim communities may also influence associational life in the Indian context. In a thesis on Bhagalpur riots, submitted to Jawaharlal Nehru University, the researcher had brought out that the leaders consider certain electoral areas as their turf, which needs to be safeguarded against any penetration. To contain influence of the leaders from the other community and also to

assert 'superiority', the local leaders patronise criminal gangs. This is done by the leaders from both the communities, and vulnerable situations like 1989 riots become the time to fight their rivalries in the public sphere. Jha, Sunil Kumar (1993), "Bhagalpur Riots: 1989", M. Phil Dissertation, New Delhi: Jawaharlal Nehru University.

References

Blomkvist, Hans and Ashok Swain (2001), "Investigating Democracy and Social Capital in India", *Economic and Political Weekly*, 36(8).

Chaterjee, Partha (2010), "The State", in Jayal, Niraja Gopal and Pratap Bhanu Mehta (eds.), 'The Oxford Companion to Politics in India', New Delhi: Oxford University Press.

——(2012), "Democracy and Capitalism in India: Pursuing Two Tocquevillean Themes", in Chaterjee, Partha and Ira Katzenlson (eds.), 'Anxieties of Democracy: Tocquevillean Reflections on India and the United States', New Delhi: Oxford University Press.

Chhibber, Pradeep K. (1999), "Democracy without Associations: Transformation of the Party System and Social Cleavages in India", New Delhi: Vistaar Publications.

Chhibber, Pradeep K. and Rahul Verma (2013), "A Platform of, by and for the Connected", *The Indian Express,* New Delhi.

Dreze, Jean and Amartya Sen (2014), "An Uncertain Glory: India and Its Contradictions", New Delhi: Penguin.

Fung, Archon (2003), "Associations and Democracy: Between Theories, Hopes and Realities", *Annual Review of Sociology*, Vol. 29.

Gutman, Amy (1998), "Freedom of Association: An Introductory Essay", in Amy Gutman (ed.), 'Freedom of Association', Princeton: Princeton University Press.

Hardgrave, Robert L., Jr. (1970), "India: Government and Politics in a Developing Nation", New York: Harcount, Brace and World.

Hasan, Zoya (2010), "Political Parties", in Jayal, Niraja Gopal and Pratap Bhanu Mehta (eds.), 'The Oxford Companion to Politics in India', New Delhi: Oxford University Press.

Hirst, Paul (1989), "The Pluralist Theory of the State: Selected Writings of G.D.H Cole, J.N. Figgis and H.J. Laski", London: Routledge.

——(1994), "Associative Democracy: New Forms of Economic and Social Governance", Cambridge: Polity Press.

Jayal, Neerja Gopal (2001), "Democracy and Social Capital in Central Himalaya: Tale of Two Villages", *Economic and Political Weekly*, 36(8).

Jha, Sunil Kumar (1993), "Bhagalpur Riots: 1989", dissertation, Jawaharlal Nehru University.

Kaviraj, Sudipta (2012), "The Empire of Democracy: Reading Indian Politics through Tocqueville" in Chaterjee, Partha and Ira Katzenlson (eds.), 'Anxieties of Democracy: Tocquevillean Reflections on India and the United States', New Delhi: Oxford University Press.

Kothari, Rajni and Rushikesh Maru (1970), "Federating for Political Interests: The Kshtriyas of Gujarat" in Rajni Kothari (ed.), 'Caste in Indian Politics', Hyderabad: Orient Longman.

Krishna, Anirudh (2002), "Enhancing Political Participation in Democracies: What is the Role of Social Capital?", *Comparative Political Studies*, 35(4).

Lijphart, Arend (2008), "The Puzzle of Indian Democracy: A Consociational Interpretation" in Arend Lijphart, 'Thinking about Democracy: Power Sharing and Majority Rule in Theory and Practice', New York: Routledge.

Mohapatra, Bishnu (2001), "Social Connectedness and Fragility of Social Capital: View from an Orissa Village", *Economic and Political Weekly*, 36(8).

Pai, Sudha (2001), "Social Capital, Panchayats and Grassroots Democracy: Politics of Dalit Assertion in Uttar Pradesh", *Economic and Political Weekly*, 36(8).

Putnam, Robert D. and Kristin A. Goss (2002), "Introduction" in Robert D. Putnam (ed.), 'Democracies in Flux', New York: Oxford University Press.

Putnam, Robert D. (2000), "Bowling Alone: The Collapse and Revival of American Community", New York: Simon & Schuster.

Putnam, Robert D., Robert Leonardi and Raffaella Nanetti (1993), "Making Democracy Work: Civic Traditions in Modern Italy", Princeton: Princeton University Press.

Rosen, George (1966), "Democracy and Economic Change in India", London: Cambridge University Press.

Rudolph, Llyod I. and Susanne Hoeber Rudolph (1968), "The

Modernity of Tradition: Political Development in India", Chicago: University of Chicago Press.

—(2008), "The Political Role of India's Caste Associations" in Llyod I. Rudolph and Susanne Hoeber Rudolph (eds.), 'Explaining Indian Democracy: A Fifty Year Perspective, 1956-2006', New Delhi: Oxford University Press.

Sandel, Michael J. (1984), "Liberalism and its Critics", Oxford: Basil Blackewell.

Sarkar, Sumit (2001), "Indian Democracy: The Historical Inheritance", in Atul Kohli (ed.), 'The Success of India's Democracy', Cambridge: Cambridge University Press.

Taylor, Charles (1995), "Invoking Civil Society" in Robert E. Goodin and Philip Pettit (eds.), 'A Companion to Contemporary Political Philosophy', Massachusetts: Blackwell Publishing.

Tocqueville, Alexis de (2007), "Democracy in America", translated by Henry Reeve, Cambridge: Sever and Francis.

Varshney, Ashutosh (2002), "Ethnic Conflict and Civic Life: Hindus and Muslims in India", New Haven and London: Yale University Press.

Verba, S. et al. (1995), "Beyond SES: A Resource Model of Political Participation", *American Political Science Review*, 89(2).

Vora, Rajendra and Suhas Palshikar (eds.) (2004), "Indian Democracy: Meanings and Practices", New Delhi: Sage Publications.

Warren, Mark E. (2001), "Democracy and Association", New Jersey: Princeton University Press.

Index